JAMES BREARLEY

A TEENAGER'S

WAR

A true story of an 18 year old lad from Huddersfield fighting during WW2 in France, Belgium, Holland and Germany with the 5th Black Watch 51st Highland Division

JAMES BREARLEY

A TEENAGER'S WAR

A true story of an 18 year old lad from Huddersfield fighting
during WW2 in France, Belgium, Holland and Germany with
the 5th Black Watch 51st Highland Division

MEREO
Cirencester

Mereo Books

1A The Wool Market Dyer Street Cirencester Gloucestershire GL7 2PR
An imprint of Memoirs Publishing www.mereobooks.com

A Teenagers War: 978-1-86151-127-0

First published in Great Britain in 2014
by Mereo Books, an imprint of Memoirs Publishing

Copyright ©2014

James Brearley has asserted his right under the Copyright Designs and Patents
Act 1988 to be identified as the author of this work.

A CIP catalogue record for this book is available from the British Library.

The address for Memoirs Publishing Group Limited can be found at
www.memoirspublishing.com

The Memoirs Publishing Group Ltd Reg. No. 7834348

The Memoirs Publishing Group supports both The Forest Stewardship Council® (FSC®) and
the PEFC® leading international forest-certification organisations. Our books carrying both the
FSC label and the PEFC® and are printed on FSC®-certified paper. FSC® is the only forest-
certification scheme supported by the leading environmental organisations including
Greenpeace. Our paper procurement policy can be found at
www.memoirspublishing.com/environment

Cover Design - Ray Lipscombe

Typeset in 11.5/16pt Plantin
by Wiltshire Associates Publisher Services Ltd. Printed and bound in Great Britain by
Printondemand-Worldwide, Peterborough PE2 6XD

PLEASE MAKE A DONATION

If you have enjoyed reading this book and wish to make a donation please forward your contribution by one of the following methods.

Bank transfer.
Account: Nat West
Account Name: Brearley J.
Account number: 51654695 sort code 60-18-10

Cheque to J Brearley, 6, Plaistow Way, Great Chishill, South Cambridgeshire, SG8 8SQ

PayPal jb@jamesbrearley.com

Charities: The beneficiaries will be The Highlanders or British Legion or any other appropriate Army Charity

I hereby promise that 100% of donations will go to the listed charities above or a Forces Charity of your choice.

James Brearley

ABOUT A TEENAGERS WAR

This is a true story about an eighteen-year-old Yorkshire lad who fought during World War II.

Until joining the 5th Black Watch 51st Highland Division he had never travelled out of Yorkshire. James Watson was my uncle however, in order to enhance the story line, Eric Holroyd is a fictional character who has been written in the context of how I believe an eighteen-year-old Yorkshire lad would handle the experience, just as James did, of the traumas of war from the beaches of Normandy, through Belgium and Holland, and finally into Germany.

All the stories and battles are correct and true as they are based on war records, James Watson's service records, soldiers' diaries and conversations with veterans of the 51st Highland Division and the family of James Watson.

Following more than two years of research, I am proud to have documented the experiences of those brave soldiers of the 51st Highland Division in the hope that the readers of this book will help carry forward the memory of all those who participated, in any way, in the Second World War.

For they made a better life for us and our children

ACKNOWLEDGEMENTS

This book is dedicated to the family of James Watson and would not have been possible without the help and generosity of the organisations and individuals who have helped the author to collate accurate information.

I wish to thank Dr. Tom Renouf, who also joined the 51st Highlands and trained with James Watson, for kindly spending hours on the phone recalling stories of the war. My thanks go to Major Ronnie Proctor and Thomas B Smyth, Archivist at The Museum of The Black Watch.

It could also not have been accomplished without the use of the Army Personnel Centre Historical Disclosures and Forces War Records.

Thanks to the late John McGregor, author of The Spirit of Angus, Chalky White from the Red Hackle Club and author Harry Duffin for his invaluable advice on presentation.

Finally, thank you to those websites who provided invaluable information relating to the subject of WW2.

Imperial War Museum	www.iwm.or.uk
The BBC	www.bbc.co.uk/history/ww2
Commonwealth War Graves	www.cwgc.org
Library and Archives of Canada	www.collectionscanada.gc.ca
Canada at War	www.canadaatwar.ca
Wikipedia	www.wikipedia.com

Contents

JAMES WATSON

James Watson was born on 19th July 1925 to Albert and Minnie Watson in Lockwood, Huddersfield in West Yorkshire.

With three elder sisters, Marion, Alma, Monam and later a younger sister Jenny, being the only boy in the family he was doted on by his loving sisters and especially his father Albert.

James was not a strong, healthy child and shortly after birth he developed tuberculosis, commonly known as 'consumption' in Victorian times. Tuberculosis is a disease of the lungs which can spread to other organs and if left untreated was usually fatal.

Lockwood was a heavily-industrial area of Huddersfield, the centre of the woollen industry.

Albert decided it was not the ideal environment for James so he decided to move to the outskirts where the air would be fresher and it would help James's breathing difficulties.

Their new home was 125 Yewtree Road, Birchencliffe, and was ideal. Surrounded by fields, rolling hills and a garden that overlooked the local cricket field. Albert bought James a black Labrador to encourage him to take walks and enjoy the village environment.

From 1930 to 1940 James attended Lindley School

where he completed his basic education, before moving to his first employment at Hopkinson's iron foundry. Maybe not the ideal place to work however Albert was a foreman of the works and managed to get James an office job.

During his early teens, James joined the Air Training Corps (ATC), also known as Air Cadets, a voluntary youth group supported by the Ministry of Defence and part of the Royal Air Force.

For most this would be an induction into the RAF prior to reaching the age of eighteen.

For James, however, this was not to be as he was told very early in the cadets that he would not qualify for the RAF due to his poor health.

Albert did not want James to apply for military service as his office job at Hopkinson's was considered an important role at home and the iron foundry was being utilised in supplying the MOD's requirements.

So, technically, James was secure in his job and he had lots of friends, including his girlfriend Rene. However, he was frustrated knowing many of his mates were joining up and because most of the conversations were about those brave young men keen to enrol and fight for the country.

Unbeknown to his father, James applied to join the Territorial Army at the recruiting office in Huddersfield on 8th April 1943, aged just seventeen and due to reach eighteen in three months' time.

On the same day he had his medical examination

which he passed as A1 and fit for general service by the medical board, signed off by H.J. Horne.

On the registration form James expressed his desire to serve in the Black Watch, Highland Regiment and was prepared to serve abroad rather than stay in the reserves. Within weeks he was instructed to go to Perth in Scotland to commence his training at the Primary Training Wing.

On 20th June 1943, he signed up with the 5th Battalion of the Black Watch and commenced infantry training.

James Watson Aged 17 years 1943

PERTH TRAINING HEADQUARTERS

This was the day I started a whole new chapter in my life. Just over a week before, I signed up for the Territorial Army Reserves in the recruiting office in Huddersfield. Completed the Army form E 531, had the medical and Captain Wilson signed the approval form for me to become an attested recruit. I was then instructed to report to (PTW) Perth Training Wing on 20th April as I had been accepted as a potential candidate by the Black Watch.

I needed to travel to Perth station where I was to be met by someone from the Black Watch. I was told that many recruits would be arriving at the same time.

Lots of my mates signed up with the TA with no specific request to join a regiment and this allowed them to go into training and await call up, if and when required.

For me I wanted to go into action and fight for my country but, more importantly, I wanted to join the

Scottish Highlanders who, to me, represented a regiment of true fighting heroes with a history second to none.

I had no sense of nervousness or fear when I said goodbye to my parents at Huddersfield Station on my way to Perth via York and Edinburgh. After all I was eighteen years old. I felt like a man and I was built like one after having played rugby since I was eleven years old. I had trained and performed as good as any age since I was sixteen years old. Yes I was mentally strong when saying goodbye, but I did have a feeling that my mother was hiding her pain inside while trying to show parental support. Dad was just nodding his head and at the same time winking at me as if to say "tha'll be all reet lad" just as he did before I would play an important rugby match.

The journey was unbelievable considering I'd never been out of Yorkshire before except for once to Blackpool and I had once on a Boys' Brigade camp to Knaresborough.

Within half an hour or so I was in York Station. What a splendid sight. I thought Huddersfield station was big but York was unbelievable, so grand with wonderful Victorian structures of cast iron and steel.

The station was very busy with both civilians and soldiers in smart uniforms. I imagined what it would be like to stand proud in my kit in just a few days' time.

I was a little confused knowing I had to change platforms so I checked with the porter where I needed to go and at the same time, as if he was interested, I told him I was on my way to Perth to join the Black Watch. The journey took a coastal route with views of the sea, passing Durham and eventually arriving into Edinburgh Waverly Station. The platform was packed with young men dressed in civilian clothes ready to board for Perth. I was soon to learn we were going to the same destination: Perth Barracks.

They were mostly Scots but even they had their different dialects between them. However I recognised the accent because at school I met a boy who moved from Glasgow to Huddersfield who he had the same melodic twang.

Finally we reached Perth Station and were met by a soldier from the Black Watch who gathered us together and walked us through the town to the barracks. On arrival we were signed in then taken to a hut that accommodated about twenty would be soldiers. I was hoping the lads would not take the piss out of me being English and accept the fact that it was my choice to join the Black Watch rather than a Yorkshire regiment.

It turned out not to be a problem at all, as I quickly inherited the nickname Yorkie and even they referred to themselves as Jocks in a friendly sort of way.

Within a short time we were ordered to line up outside to receive a briefing from our instructors Sergeant Alexander and Corporal Amos.

It was then to the Quartermasters store to be issued with our initial kit.

In the large room were rows of tables with staff lined up behind and, like a factory conveyor belt, they dished out the goodies. Being a little cocky when it came to shirts (I think they called it a blouse), I requested a fourteen and a half collar, "no starch please", which went down like a lead balloon with the chappy giving them out. It amused the lad next to me who could only give out a snigger of laughter, being cautious of not showing disrespect to the staff.

The guy then asked where I was from as it was obvious I was not a Jock, so I replied "Brighouse, lad", thinking he would have no idea where Brighouse was, but he quickly replied "I'm from Birchencliffe, just up the road from Brighouse.

"My name is James Watson, who are you?"

I just could not believe that on my first day there was a lad from Huddersfield standing right next to me and my immediate reaction was that I was going to like this man and hoped we were going to be together in days to come. Better two Yorkies than one.

By the time we reached the end of the line and held out our kit bags for the servers to fill them we had been issued with shirts, trousers, capes, jackets, braces and even shaving kits, already a heavy load to carry back to our huts.

One thing I do recall is the fact that everything appeared to fit us well, as if the staff could tell at a glance the correct size. In addition they paid careful attention to the correct boot size. This is something they knew would be vitally important in the future.

We were told very clearly by Corporal Amos that we must take care of our issue and if we were to lose anything whatsoever we would have to pay for replacements.

Despite being tired having travelled up from Yorkshire and had a lot to take in on my first day, I was excited to learn that we were to gather this evening for dinner in the dining hall.

The hall was gigantic and they served a really well-proportioned, tasty dinner.

This gave us all chance to chat and get to know each other, the guys were very friendly and I had a feeling I would settle in here with no reservations.

James was quickly referred to as Jimmy, a popular name in Scotland, however he settled for Jim and before the end of the evening became Yorkie Jim.

I was pleased that Jim and I shared the same billet as we had so much in common, including our love for Huddersfield Town. Jim in particular had two football heroes: Billy Price and Jimmy Glazzard.

As we were now both away from home, we would rely on newspapers and the radio to keep us updated on Town news.

After dinner it was back to the hut for a well-deserved sleep.

Early the next morning we familiarised ourselves with the surroundings in Perth Barracks before attending a lecture on the history of the 51st Highland Regiment and in particular their actions in the Great War and the current conflict.

The 51st were fighting in Tunisia and Algeria and we had daily updates on their progress, the news being mixed. The could be talking about going to the cinema, bathing parties and football matches yet only days ago endured heavy casualties, including the death of Sergeant McBride and two captains badly wounded. That month we had lost twenty boys from the 5th Battalion alone. History shows just how great the battalion is and how their contribution to the war effort is second to none.

One of the instructors told us non-Scots: "you must absorb, respect and commit to the history and tradition of the Highland Regiment in order to qualify for the accolade of becoming a Jock."

For Jim and I this was not a problem as we were already totally committed to applying for the honour. We then had a detailed instruction on how to take care of our kit and how important is was to keep it in pristine condition as weekly and random kit inspections would take place and we were told "if you don't want the glasshouse treatment, keep your kit perfect."

Woe betides any man whose folded blankets showed an edge or whose collections of brushes were not aligned perfectly during inspection.

Our uniforms were checked for fitting reasonably well, we were presented with our military number, dog tags and instructed never to remove them from around our necks as it may become the only form of identification. We were given our pay books and informed that we would receive two shillings a day for ourselves and a further one shilling would go to our parents.

Then it was off to the armoury to collect our Lee Enfield rifles and bayonets, the serial numbers of which were registered to our names. Again something one must never lose sight of: your weapon.

We had no idea how the rifle functioned as we had never handled one before but were told "don't worry you will soon learn."

Finally we were marched off to the one-style barber shop which was fun as within hours we all looked the same. No room for personal preference!

Our next job was to parcel up all our personal belongings as they would be returned to our homes.

We were allowed to keep small personal objects. Jim kept his fountain pen, a pocket torch and a small Union Jack.

Sergeant then informed us that tomorrow morning we would continue our initiation training in a more physical manner by a workout in the gym, then followed by an eight mile route march in full kit.

Bright and early next morning the first physical training session commenced, but to be honest I found it quite easy due to my rugby background. However, the corporal told me not to get complacent as this was just an easing-in process and the eight miles would soon become sixteen miles.

Training at Perth was precise excellence; our

superiors knew exactly what was required to make every one of us a fighting force. In addition, we had lectures on current affair and were taught how to cook not just for ourselves but with the fourteen-man food pack supplied when on the battlefield.

After a short while of initial training we were allowed to go outside the barracks to discover life in the beautiful city of Perth, which we had only previously seen during route marches. Also it was the first chance we had to celebrate Jim's 18th birthday on 19th July.

One can guess that the initial objectives were to find the girlie spots in town to see what chance there was of tasting the local talent. Obviously we had it drummed into us that whatever we got up to in town, at all times we were representing the Black Watch and under no circumstances must we put the reputation of the battalion into disrepute.

When allowed out of camp we needed to remember basic rules that sounded school boyish but were there to project the fine image of the battalion.

They included:

- *Outer garments such as greatcoats are either worn completely buttoned up or else taken off entirely.*

- *Hands will be kept out of pockets.*

- *Uniforms should never be mixed with civilian attire.*

- *Soldiers will not lean against walls but will either sit in an appropriate place or stand erect.*

- *Thank people who pay compliments on your display or your appearance.*

- *Don't argue with people who say that you have done something wrong, even if they are incorrect.*

The local people were wonderful, kind, friendly and sometimes even invited you into their homes for meals and drinks.

The city, which sits on the River Tay and is known as the Fair City, was soon to become our temporary home. We were surprised to learn that Perth was not just the home of the Jocks but also Americans who were stationed at the air base and many Poles who were being trained locally. We used a cafe for soldiers run by women volunteers and a cheap Italian cafe, I think it was called Rabalotti, where you could get a cup of Bovril for a penny. We met up with some guys from Tyneside Scottish who were living next door to our barracks in an old dye works known to the locals as Campbell's Dye House.

We were invited to look at their place and soon realised how grand our huts where in comparison to their cramped, bunk-bed conditions.

Jim and I were just getting to know the place when we were granted weekend leave and both decided to train it back to Huddersfield.

We did not meet over the weekend, needing to spend time with our families, however we travelled back to Perth by train together, both of us eager to get back to our mates. Jim told me he had managed to watch

Huddersfield Town beat Bradford Park Avenue 7-4, his hero Billy Price scoring four goals, so that was the main topic of conversation during our journey back.

We spent a further five months based in and around Perth completing the intense infantry training which included time north of Perth surviving in tents on the cold moorlands and learning map-reading, trench-digging and general combat skills.

We had an interesting lecture on the Atlantic Wall, something I did not even know existed, however it was very informative and proved how determined the Germans were in both attack and defence, in preparation for the future.

The Atlantic Wall was the name given to a massive coastal defensive structure, being built on Hitler's orders, which stretches all the way from Norway, along the Belgium and French coastline to the Spanish border.

It covered a distance of 1,670 miles and formed the main part of Hitler's 'Fortress Europe'. The wall is being built to repel any Allied attack on Nazi-occupied Europe wherever it is planned.

The building of the wall started in 1942 and work was still in progress.

Artillery emplacements were supported with machine-gun posts and other artillery emplacements, built inland to give the wall some form of protection if the expected Allied landings took place.

Beaches along the northern coastline of France were strewn with anti-tank and anti-vehicle obstacles known as 'Rommel's Teeth'.

Many of these had mines attached to them so that at high tide both the 'teeth' and the mines will not been seen by an invading force keen to get onto the beaches. Six-million mines had been laid on beaches in Northern France.

Many thousands of French men were forced to work on the Atlantic Wall as part of an arrangement between the Vichy government and the Albert Speer's Organisation Todt.

There was no choice for the French and other foreigners. The conditions were terrible but they earned a slave labour wage which helped them feed their families which was better than being in a concentration camp.

The most heavily-constructed batteries were around the north and west coasts of France. Their primary purpose was to defend against an Allied invasion, but its massive guns were also used against shipping in the English Channel and against Dover itself. They fired thousands of shells at targets in the channel or against Dover or Folkestone, this part of Kent now known as 'Hell Fire Corner'. I am not sure why we had this lecture, maybe to give us knowledge of the task ahead, but for sure it was not a confidence booster.

On October 1943 Jim gave me some shocking news. I was in the billet cleaning my kit when he came in with his head facing the floor and said, "Sorry mate, bad news. I have just been informed I am being transferred for further training with the 4th Black Watch in Chichester, Sussex."

For the past seven months he had become my best friend, closeness I had never experienced before, we were like brothers something neither of us had at home.

After about an hour I was called in to see the sergeant who was seated in his office, I stood to attention in front of his desk he quickly cut to the chase by announcing, "Lad, you're going to Chichester next week". He had no idea what joy was going through my mind as I replied, "Very well, Sergeant."

Back in the billet Jim was sat reading a book and I wanted to tell him I was moving to Norfolk or somewhere just to wind him up. But I could see he was unhappy with the move so I decided to tell him: "Guess what mate? We are off to Chichester on 20th October" We both skipped around the bunks singing "We're off to Chichester!"

Great news, we were going to Chichester together.

Perth Barracks Scotland

Supplied by the Black Watch Museum
Typical accommodation at Perth

James in uniform 1943

The Black Watch Fabric Patch

The Black Watch Badge

PREPARING FOR D-DAY

Although we had no idea at the time that we were being prepared for the invasion of Europe, our superiors in the higher ranks knew exactly what was going to be needed and so training reflected precisely that.

The experiences since 1939 had been taken into consideration and the knowledge of future battle plans was obviously the key to our preparation.

We were sorry to leave Perth, having settled in well to the army life in and around the Fair City.

Around twenty of us were escorted to Perth Station, accompanied by a corporal, where we boarded a train to London King's Cross.

We carried our full kit including our rifles and haversacks stuffed with sandwiches to satisfy our hunger during the journey.

Arriving at King's Cross, the corporal hurried us along to the underground station. This was a tricky movement owing to the fact that we wore our greatcoats and carried fully-loaded kitbags. Up and down stairs, through narrow passages, we were knackered by the time we boarded the tube.

We already knew most of the guys from Queen's Barracks so the trip was full of camaraderie. We did not get a chance to see any of London, despite it being the first visit for both of us, however we were too pre-occupied with our forthcoming arrival at Chichester to lament it too much.

We had little time to settle in our new surrounding before having briefing lectures, giving an outline of what was required of us.

For the first time we were amongst a wider range of ages, as some of the guys were around thirty-years-old and had already been in service so had lots of advice to share.

Infantry training was based upon learning to operate as a battalion alongside the 4th Black Watch where we experienced various realistic battle situations.

We were also involved with 21st Army Group including Operation Scheme Eagle, learning to survive in freezing conditions. We just could not believe it when this operation was based on the Yorkshire moors, less than 20 miles from home.

Our superiors wanted to try out various tactics and movements to see how they would work in real battle situations.

We would huddle in slit trenches, almost paralysed by the freezing cold, knowing we were being observed by the trainers.

On our return to base they would then let us know all the things we did wrong and how we would have been dead men had it been a real life situation.

Jim jokingly suggested we sneak out to watch Town play Crewe Alexander. He was over the moon later when he heard they had won 8-0 and Billy Price had scored seven and Jimmy Glazzard one.

Training continued, moving around the country until we were granted Christmas leave on 14th December. This was a golden opportunity to rush back to Yorkshire for two weeks to our families and friends, it seemed ages since we had been back, having been very close to home when training up north.

Christmas was spent enjoying the family get togethers as we both took time to visit and meet each other's parents for the first time.

I went to Birchencliffe and had a few pints with Jim and his Dad in the Grey Horse and Jim came down to our place when we did a pub crawl in Rastrick.

My parents were well impressed with Jim and were constantly quizzing him on what was going to happen next.

To be honest we hadn't a clue only to say we are being trained for the future.

We were both proud to show off our uniforms, which often got us a free beer in the locals.

At the end of December we had to report back to HQ where there was a relaxed atmosphere and lots to catch up on with our mates, all comparing our holiday adventures. Nothing much went on throughout January until 13th February 1944 when we were posted back to the 5th Black Watch as they were operating in High Wycombe. On arrival there was absolute chaos as unbeknown to us the day after, Valentine's Day, the 153

Brigade were to be inspected by the boss: General Sir B. L. Montgomery.

Monty inspected the Brigade and actually spoke to some privates, everyone in awe of perhaps the most famous person we will ever meet.

We only got a glimpse of him until he began to address the Brigade when we could hear and see the man as he spoke.

He opened by saying he was glad to have the 51st Highland division once again under his command. He called for an increase in the tempo of training for the formidable tasks which lay ahead.

Jim and I chatted later about our feelings that very soon we will be going to Europe.

The camp included many officers and OR's who had just returned from the Battle of Alamein, Tripoli, Tunisia, Algeria, Sicily and Malta.

Their homecoming in November 1943 was by sea on the USS Argentina to Liverpool.

The battalion had been reduced to around 600 and would be increased to 900 before any future roles, Jim and I being two of the reinforcements.

Future training would include those veterans so it was great for us novices to work alongside the professionals.

No sooner had we got over the excitement of Monty's visit when our CO informed us that on 23rd February we were to be inspected by a very important person: Colonel-in Chief, HM Queen Elizabeth.

All was well prepared as we waited around for her arrival. It was a dull day, it looked like rain but that would not interfere with any arrangements.

She arrived in an entourage of elite cars and was quickly surrounded by the officers in charge who led her to be presented to the brigade.

She slowly walked down the line nodding her head in approval and actually spoke to some guys as I could see her getting closer and closer to me and Jim.

She came so close, standing only two paces in front of me, but she did not say anything and we were told not to speak unless she asked a question.

We were told to address her as 'Your Highness' but only if she spoke first.

I wanted to hold my hand out to shake her hand but that would have put me in the glass house.

I wish our Mums and Dads could see us now and the lads in Brighouse would not believe a word I tell them when I get home.

We could not believe how petite she was, she had a warm smile, very confident stature and she just chatted away to the nervous personnel of all ranks.

She had the quality in making people feel at ease, a wonderful lady.

After an inspection she addressed the Battalion, a record was made as follows:

Colonel Thomson and all ranks of the 5th Battalion, The Black Watch.

It is will great pleasure to see on parade again the Battalion with which, through my family, I have special association. When I last visited you your training was at an end, you stood on the threshold of active service with all its hazards and its adventures. As I look at you today you have converted great promise into even greater performance in Egypt, across North Africa and in Sicily. Some of those who set out with you stand in the ranks no more, they will not be forgotten. No doubt those who now fill their places will carry forward the outstanding reputation of this fine Battalion.

No one knows what may be before you, but whatever it may entail, I leave in your hands.

I bid you all God speed.

Before leaving the Queen was cheered and listened to the Pipes and Drums playing her favourite tune "Scotland the Brave."

"Well Jim," I said, "I feel so moved, so motivated that I think I am ready to fight the fight. Monty and the Queen's visit must tell you we are off pretty soon. What a fantastic day."

Once the Queen had left, while we were all still in line, the CO announced that Monty was returning in a couple of days.

The next day came with the same well-practised routine as the V.I.P's arrived but not just Monty, he was accompanied by Allied Supreme Commander, General Dwight Eisenhower and Air Chief Marshal Tedder.

After the inspection they all spent time talking to groups of the battalion and finally the massed Pipes and Drums played "Beating Retreat."

The next day the Moderator of the Church of Scotland was shown around by the CO and Padre Nicol but there was no need for a formal inspection.

The final day of February we were training on Stoke Common when it was announced that a very special guest was about to arrive, General Sir Arthur Wauchope and alongside him was HM King George VI, yes, the King of England.

The King was more formal and he did not appear to be as interested as the Queen, maybe because he is a man he looked like the leader, walked like a military man, never smiled, didn't look anyone in the eye, never spoke to the guys in line and with respect gave the impression he was in a rush to another appointment.

This suited us because we were terrified he may ask us a question and I would not have a clue what to say if he had.

He did, however, take the time to congratulate us on our performance since the start of the war and mentioned the bravery of the 51st Highlanders in France in 1940. He went on to say he hoped that the reformation would continue to maintain the fine historical repetition of the Division.

The CO confirmed to the King that reinforcements had brought the battalion back to strength over establishment to 45 Officers and 863 OR's.

What a week, only a few days ago we thought we had met the most important man ever, but since then to have been in the company of the King and Queen was just unbelievable.

We must be off to the war soon.

Back to training, where the concentration was on tactics to be used in wooded country and small fields, simulating European conditions.

The battalion practised night advances, consolidation, patrolling and defence against counter attack. This was followed by a basic understanding of wireless technology (WT) and weaponry skills on ranges.

We practised river crossing on the Thames, and familiarised ourselves with boarding and disembarking on tricky landing surfaces, including thick, muddy conditions.

Despite intensive training we still had time for sports activities, including football.

The battalion had its own team known as the Incognitos, they played to quite a high standard, too good for us to be considered.

They would play against other battalions and it was far from being a friendly game as battalion pride was at stake, great to watch especially when we won.

Basically we were kept on our toes and time flew fast as spring approached.

Early in April we moved to Wethersfield, Essex so it was back to hutted accommodations, it was clean and spacious, however there was a weird smell about the place as it carried the odour similar to that of mould. This became obvious when we were told it was formally a mushroom factory.

The camp was close to a heavy bomber base and their nightly missions made undisturbed sleep difficult which gave us further inclinations that the crunch was rapidly approaching.

News reached us that American and British air forces were successfully hitting key targets in France, demobilising German defences, all forms of communication and transport.

We would share our letters from our loved ones at home, knowing they must be aware of the likelihood of forthcoming action in Europe.

All letters in and out of camp were censored, with bits cut out if we were giving or receiving too much information. I intended to keep a diary as a keepsake when I returned home but was told it was against the rules as it would carry useful information if captured by the enemy. We listened to Worker's Playtime most days and kept up to date with the latest songs by Vera Lynn and Ann Shelton and naturally got the Town football results. Training now included street-fighting techniques and searching bombed buildings of Whitechapel in

London. This included entering a street in search of the enemy and making the area safe,

Unlike field battles one needed to be lightly clad without the back pack, pick and shovel which catch in window frames and tight positions, we would carry a rifle, maybe a Bren, a supply of grenades and always be aware that the enemy could just around the corner in readiness to take you.

The locals included Cockney Dockers and families who had survived the worst of the blitz yet retained a great sense of friendliness and community spirit.

They referred to us as Jocks not knowing the difference between Yorkshire and Scottish accents but they were generous to a fault with their offers of drinks, always accompanied with a piss-taking sense of humour.

A new part of training was making our acquaintance with various modes of transport and fighting vehicles including Landing Craft Tanks (LCT's), Tracked amphibious vehicles (Buffaloes), Flame-throwing tanks (Crocodiles),

Small track vehicles (Carriers), amphibious vehicles (DUKWs), armoured personnel carriers (Kangaroos), anti-tank guns (Pheasant), Carriers with flamethrowers (Wasps) and Wide track vehicles for soft ground or snow (Weasels). Although we were not expected to operate the vehicles for sure we had to recognise their functions.

Exercises were held with the Royal Navy Volunteer

Reserve in coastal waters around Harwich where the beaches were similar to the ones in Northern Europe.

In previous conflicts at war the US Marines had experimented with landing craft to make amphibious assaults on beaches.

In 1941, the British further developed the idea with the Landing Ship Tank (LST) and the Landing Craft, Tank (LCT).

The LST is a large vessel as big as a light cruiser, it is 327-feet long and flat-bottomed, it could be difficult to handle in high seas, but it could be almost beached, when the doors in the bow would then swing aside, a ramp would be lowered and dozens of tanks and trucks would drive ashore from the hold.

It could also carry small landing craft on its deck.

The LCT was smaller, 110 feet long, and could carry between four and eight tanks, which would be landed via a ramp. Although, again, it was flat-bottomed, it was more stable than the LST, and could handle rough seas. When the US joined us in the war they took over the production of LSTs and LCTs so today they have been well tested the only concerned being the handling in rough seas. Thanks to the Americans we have other Landing Craft such as the Medium (LCM), and the Landing Craft infantry (LCI). The LCI is 160 feet long and will carry two-hundred men who will be discharged down ramps either side of the bow. Then there was the DUKW, or 'Duck'. This is a standard US two-and-a-half ton truck fitted with floatation tanks and propellers.

Guess the lectures worked as I think I know a lot about landing craft. By this time everyone knew that they were to be part of the invasion force, when and where was not known, so the guessing game dominated conversation. Two new officers arrived from the Canadian Black Watch and some from the American army, again giving concern that the day is imminent.

17th May 1944 we moved from Wethersfield to S1 Camp, Tilbury. The weather was fine and we had time to relax and enjoy the camp facilities. Some guys were playing a form of softball, new to us, but became very popular as we learned the rules similar to rounder's played with a baseball bat and leather ball. We were granted a 24 hour pass but decide we were too far away to go back to Huddersfield so we spent some time in London, only to learn on the 26th May all leave was cancelled and we had probably blown the last chance to see our families.

The same day the camp was closed, a lock-in situation, totally secured with wire fencing and arm guarded from both sides. The weather was really good as we spent time having fun, whenever girls passed they would receive rousing cheers and catcalls from the lads.

We were given French Francs today which removes any doubts as to our next destination.

The next day a full briefings commenced on the planned Operation Overlord.

Maps of the French coastline were produced and tabled sand models used to show landing tactics.

We were informed that the battalion would come under the command of the 3rd Canadian Division during the D-Day landings.

We now knew there was a job to be done and nothing was overlooked in the physical or mental preparation for our coming role.

For us two eighteen year olds from Yorkshire we had enjoyed the training we felt confident and proud, however, truth known we were absolutely terrified.

Trench Training in Scotland

River crossing training in Scotland

A landing craft during operations training

General Montgomery inspects 51st Highland Division Feb. 1944

Supplied by the Black Watch Museum HRH Queen Elizabeth
visited the troops prior to D-Day

HRH King George inspecting 51st Highlanders

OPERATION OVERLORD

D-DAY NORMANDY LANDINGS

On Saturday 3rd June we boarded LCI's at Tilbury Docks and moved into the Thames Estuary carrying about two hundred of us, of all ranks and men from rifle companies and 5/7th Gordon's.

During the day the weather became very windy making movement very difficult and uneasy as we took shelter from the land close to Southend. We were told that due to the weather deteriorating we were unlikely to move that evening and to make ourselves as comfortable as possible in the cramped choppy conditions.

Overnight the weather remained the same and there was talk of the venture being cancelled, something we did not want as we were prepared and did not want a rerun, we just wanted to get on with it.

We had food rations including, soup, meat and veg stew and hot tea was supplied with various other goodies.

Having now had almost two days hanging around, early Monday morning, 5th June we began to move slowly forward, through the misted estuary around the Kent coast, into the channel.

The progress continued quite slowly until the darkness of the stormy night, when we increased speed joining a vast armada heading full speed for the Normandy beaches.

During the crossing a "Mr-Know-It-All" sitting close by began to recall the battalion's misfortune in St Valery-en-Caux during the retreat at the end of May 1940.

He explained in detail that the 51st Division were about 80 miles from Dunkirk retreating from the Germans under French command, heading for the beaches in a hope to get home as 300,000 soldiers had been plucked off the beaches earlier.

The battalion had little fighting resources left, lacking the ammunition and equipment to tackle the well-supplied Germans.

Some elements of the division managed to escape to La Havre and on to England, but most of the 51st found themselves in St Valery being pounded by artillery and surrounded by Rommel's tanks.

The French had already waved the white flags and surrendered in early June which resulted in the loss of 10,000 British men.

Churchill let us down, said "Mr-Know-It-All", as most of the battalion were either killed or are currently in POW camps. Churchill trusted the French and failed to send further boats to Dunkirk, blaming it on the bad weather and the fact that the Germans were bombing our ships in the Channel.

"Mr Know it All" closed by saying "let's see what happens when we arrive on the beaches of France this time"

This was not a debate we needed to hear at this stage of the operation.

Sergeant Crombie tactfully chipped in to say, "Listen men, St Valery was a different kettle of fish to what the private has just said is a fact, however, this time it's the Germans who are retreating we are just going to spank their arses.

"You have seen the Allied planes over the skies they are forcing the Germans inland to make sure we have clear beaches on arrival, there will be little resistance by the time we arrive.

"We have 10,000 aircraft deployed in Operation Overlord, they are bombing key targets, dropping paratroopers, towing gliders, carrying airborne troops and are protecting the airspace above us right now. We already have forces ahead of us clearing mines and making sure we have a safe landing, there is nothing to worry about.

"The tactics of battle are decided by those upstairs all you have to do is keep your nose clean, look after yourself , remember your training and do as you are bloody well told and you will be home by Christmas". The Jocks started to sing with full harmony which changed the atmosphere with songs like Auld Lang Syne, I belong to Glasgow, when some soloist came up with

My Bonnie lies over the ocean
My Bonnie lies over the sea
My Bonnie lies over the ocean
Bring back my Bonnie to me

Just about everyone joined in with
Bring back, bring back, bring back my Bonnie to me

The Padre gave out a load clear message with The Lord's Prayer something that hit the hearts of everyone whether you were a believer or not.

My mind was like a coiled spring, one minute enjoying the buzz and total excitement, then having a deeper thought about what we were really doing and what was about to happen.

Externally I am as strong as an ox, singing, joining in with the macho comments, sharing out the fags, but inside, I must be honest, I am terrified. It's like it was my first day at school.

Meanwhile, as daylight crept in we could see the incredible sight of every kind of vessel from battleships, destroyers, cargo ships and small sea craft all steaming in the same direction.

Some were towing barrage balloons, keeping away potential air attacks but as of yet no enemy aircraft were visible. As the sergeant told us earlier, we could see waves of Allied aircraft thundering towards the targets on land.

Adrenalin was flowing it was a sight I will never forget, there were literally thousands of vessels approaching the beaches.

As land approached at around 7a.m. the sea was choppy and we wondered how far we would have to wade, the shoreline was crowded with small vessels as we ran into what can only be described as a traffic jam.

We could see thousands of men from every direction ready to plunge into the cold choppy waters.

The first assault troops stormed ashore in order to overcome beach defences and secured the area very quickly. Tanks and other vehicles were being unloaded on Juno Beach, but due to the bottleneck situation it would appear it could be hours before our turn to land would take place.

I began to feel vulnerable amongst all those vessels parked in the sea like sitting ducks, waiting to be blasted by the enemy.

The Germans were obviously aware that something big was happening, though that didn't take much calculation because there were thousands and thousands and thousands of ships out there in front of them.

The corvettes, the destroyers and the landing ship rockets were all starting their bombardment, and the bombardment was absolutely colossal.

Thousands of shells were whizzing over the top as we came into shore and the din was absolutely deafening, indescribable.

All types of craft were firing, even the landing craft that were coming in with tanks were firing their guns actually in the landing craft to help with the bombardment or at targets that they could see they could hit.

We were supplied with waterproof, waist-high waders to protect our lower regions, yet we still had our full kit and weapons to carry above water.

Landing crafts were ferrying back and forth but still leaving men to wade waist deep to the shore, the beach was crowded with soldiers being directed to their next destination.

Some landing crafts had collided with mines. Although we were told the beach had been cleared, you could see bodies floating in the waves.

We could not see any response from the Germans on the beaches, however, further inland we could see smoke and hear explosions from the Allies hitting targets from the sea bombardments.

It was early that evening of the 6th June when ramps were dropped and we entered the chilly waters up to our waists and waded onto the beaches making sure our kit was protected from the choppy sea.

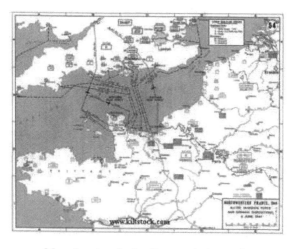

Map showing the landings and air attacks

Trucks being loaded at East India docks.

The Canadians boarding in Southampton

Southampton docks packed with vessels

Southhampton docks packed with vessels

On our way joining a vast armada

IWM A23997 -   Our Allies American and Canadian troops heading
out to Normandy

Floating harbours towed in to aid landings following the first arrivals. Supplied by Collectionscanada.gc.ca

We entered the sea, a most frightening sight ahead.

Troops landing at Juno Beach 6 June 1944

Troops desperately wading to shore

An incredible site the beaches full with troops and vehicles.
Supplied by Naval Historical Centre USA

Many troops and vehicles had problems getting ashore
Supplied by Naval Historical Centre USA

IWM OWIL 449 - Sadly we could see bodies in the
water and some on the beach

IWM B5027 - Fortunately our first sight of
the enemy was German prisoners.

What the nation would read on the headlines 7th June 1944

Our parents would read the Yorkshire Post

JUNO BEACH

6TH JUNE 1944 NORMANDY FRANCE

We were informed where to assemble just clear of the beach as the CO made contact with HQ, 3rd Canadian Division to request orders.

Jim and I still felt confident and there was a good feeling around the lads with little complaining from the usual moaners.

Despite our boys having a reasonably safe landing, as we left the beaches onto hard ground and looked back to the waters we could see many had run into difficulties and never made it to land.

Small crafts were picking up the casualties and transferring them to the hospital ships before heading homeward.

Apart from our lads getting soaked and some equipment lost, no harm was done.

The army was a few miles inland but all credit to those who, a few hours before, had lifted the mines so we were able to follow along white taped paths to a field a mile or so from the beach.

Our first face-to-face sighting of the enemy was our lads marching German prisoners in the opposite direct towards the beaches maybe they were being sent to England.

They looked shattered, heads down; most with hands on their heads. Some of them looked younger than us, many of their uniforms in tatters.

I couldn't help but think what was going through their minds. Would they be thinking the war is over for them? Maybe they were thinking they would be lined up and shot. Whatever, they must have been thinking about their loved ones just as we were, and to a degree I pitied them.

This sight reinforced our belief that the end of the war was nearing.

We were ordered to proceed to Banvilles which was only about 4 miles away.

As we marched in extended files we passed the bombed out shoreline houses through narrow lanes we saw no sight of civilians or the fighting enemy.

All around were the signs of previous air and sea bombardment, yet other than our voices there was an air of peacefulness as the evening was drawing to an end.

Some French farmers, who had refused to leave their properties, greeted us with offers of homebrew cider. Not understanding a word they were saying we received their gifts with the limited French we could come up with.

The cider was as good as any pint of Webster's bitter we had in Huddersfield.

In just over one hour we arrived on the outskirts of the little village of Branville, where we took rest for the night.

Amazing news from the corporal confirmed that the headcount had resulted in only one soldier from the 5th Battalion not making it to Banville.

We were also informed that an estimated 150,000 troops would have landed, or were about to, on the various beaches of Normandy.

The heavy casualties came from those early arrivals, the brave Americans and Canadians who had paved the way for us.

However, during the night the sounds of air attacks by the Luftwaffe bombing the beaches gave us concern about those troops behind us, yet no ground attacks were evident.

The Americans were parachuting men from aircraft and gliders ahead of us.

Jim had been assigned as the batman for one of the captains, good news for Jim as it also gave him an increase in perks.

My only concern is that maybe this would split us up when we had spent more than a year together. The position of batman was regarded as a good move by privates, as many were promoted much quicker due to their awareness around the officers.

It may also exempt him from more onerous duties and often get better rations and other favours from his officer.

In terms of battle situations nothing changes as officers of the 5th expose themselves to the same dangers as any man in the troop.

Your captain would give his life for you and vice versa.

Our next orders came that we would march to Beny-sur-Mer while under the command of 8th Canadian Brigade.

The plan was to attack Douvre la Delivande from the North West and clear the road East of Beny-sur-Mer and that we should be aware of German snipers on route.

Before arriving at Delivande we were attacked with the enemy firing from the woodland on our right. Fortunately we had support from Sherman tanks that fired into the woods forcing the enemy to retreat even further into the heavy woodland, the enemy only returning small arm fire.

We were told to affix bayonets and enter the woods ready for one to one battle.

The noise echoed through the trees, my heart was beating like a drum as this was our first taste of real fighting.

Suddenly from the rear we were ordered to stop firing, more than one voice screaming "stop firing, stop firing".

Within seconds we could hear English voices deep in the woodland giving the same orders to stop firing. On our first occasion into combat, it was not the enemy we were killing it was the Canadians. The only consolation, they fired first.

They had previously attempted to take out a German radar station and found the surrounding fields full of mines so decided to retreat to cover in the woods.

A real cock-up of communications as they thought

we were Germans retreating from the woods they had held earlier.

Sad to learn that both the 5th and the Canadians had causalities, we lost 4 men and 3 injured, not the ideal start to the invasion but for sure lessons were learnt in relation to communication.

The Canadian commander decided that the radar station must be captured as it was too important to bypass.

The revised plan was for Sherman tanks and Blockbusters to go through the wired fencing and minefields and make a clearway for us to attack. We were to leave the wooded area and take cover behind a long ridge and wait further orders.

In went the two Sherman's and Blockbusters, one Blockbuster blew up a mine, Gerry was prepared and saw them off with anti-tank guns then set fire to a Sherman, forcing the other tank to return damaged. Orders followed to return to the woodland, now known as Radar Wood, and take cover.

The Canadian commander decided it was too big a job for us to handle at the moment and requested further orders from HQ as they may instruct HMS Belfast to bombard the station. This plan was aborted so the battalion remained in the wood as it afforded good protection.

Our orders followed to advance to St Aubin as 152 Brigade would take over our position in Radar Wood. We later discovered that the radar station was a very important target, when it was taken a month later. It was the headquarters of the 8th Grenadier Regiment with underground stores of ammunition and 200 Germans were taken.

Too big a job for us to have captured and perhaps we were lucky only to have lost two men but many were injured.

So Jim and I have experienced a true battle situation, much different to training as we have seen death at first hand.

We moved to St Aubin d'Arquenay to take over from the Lincolnshire Regiment when we met up with 3rd British Division under the command of Major General Thomas Rennie someone we had knowledge of as he was well known throughout the battalion during training lectures.

Our CO informed that we were now under the command of the 6th Airborne Division who were holding the ground east of the River Orne an area where they had landed via gliders and aircraft.

Our job was to cross the river and secure a firm base South-East of Herouvillette, allowing the Gordon's to exploit South-East to Touffreville and Sannerville. A long discussion took place on how we would implement the orders given until Sergeant informed us "change of plan lads we are going to be more useful elsewhere"

Still under 6th Airborne command they needed us to fill gaps in their line between Chateau St Come, Breville and Amfreville and come under the command of 3rd Para Brigade.

The more experienced members of the 5th had heard that this was a hot spot and we were likely to have a tough time there when our training would be put to good use.

On the 10th June a radio message was sent to our Major Dunn to move to an RV (Rendezvous) on the Herouvillette to Le Mesnil road then on to the HQ of 9th Parachute Battalion. On arrival it was agreed that we would advance to Breville at first light, not giving us much time to take in any planning to complete the instructions.

Jim and I were easy on the orders but again the older lads were saying this is going to be shit lads, we have only seen unimportant little villages so far, but just look at the numbers here and just sense the tension of the Officers as they discuss the situation, they can't agree with each other, they know what's coming.

A restless night, due to the unknown, lots of activity around us and in the distance. Jim, being a batman, out of hearing from the others told me that he had overheard conversations between officers and they thought it was premature to advance to Breville as the battalion needed more time to brief the lads and plan accordingly.

First light on the 11th June, Major Dunn led the battalion out of St Aubin as we crossed the bridges over the canal and river heading for Breville.

No problems so far as everything was quiet until we were held up by a report to say there were snipers ahead and one captain had been shot, fortunately only wounded. Slowly moving forward we were led by a Regiment Intelligence officer along a muddy lane until we reached a sunken part of the road very near Chateau St Come, yet offering some protection. By now it was dark making it very difficult under the muddy conditions to see where your feet were planted. The CO was waiting for reports as to our next move, which was to cross the fields and enter Breville from the South-East side.

Until then we posted sentries in a hope we could rest peacefully until dawn. At 3a.m. the Para Patrol reported to our CO that they had come across snipers who had fired at them just ahead of the crossroads, but considered that although they did not enter the village, Breville was not strongly held and it was OK to advance.

Based on the report from the Para Patrol we were ordered to prepare to advance at 4.30 a.m. that morning.

Exactly on time, gathered together, we climbed up the muddy banks and moved forward across two fields. As we reached a hedgerow we encountered a burst of automatic gunfire from the woods on our left hand side, hitting an officer.

He remained standing, as if wounded but under control, and was able to shout out orders.

The hedgerow offered good cover until we spotted an orchard ahead, also giving cover, only a field away.

Right now all was quiet so it was assumed that the village was being protected by a few snipers. As we advanced only about 40 yards all hell let loose under intense fire from ahead and machine gun fire from overhead then from the right, the only way was to rush for cover to the other side of the field.

We returned fire only in a defensive manner, whilst we attempted to run for cover or lie down in a hope we would not be hit. Then Gerry started to hit the field with mortar bombs with white-hot shrapnel shattering everything around it.

Jim and I had been separated in the mayhem but looking around our guys were either dead or still digging in the muddy soil hoping they would not be hit and praying that the attack would soon end. I could hear tanks from the distant rear as I prayed they were our lads who would give us a fighting chance. I could see some of the boys moving for further cover to the right of the field so I decided to follow them, looking back there were lots of static bodies still lying in the field with screams of pain pounding in my head.

Myself and a handful of men proceeded back to the crossroads where we knew further cover was available, but on arrival we were hit again by withering enemy fire, dropping in numbers. It was a matter of self-preservation.

Our only choice was to get back to base as there was no way we could advance without further casualties, they were picking us off like fairground ducks.

By the time we got back to 3rd Para we learned that orders had been sent to others to retreat and report to base as there was no chance of winning this battle. It was time to recover and count our losses and for the CO to take orders based on the strength and capabilities of the remaining platoon.

Our boys began to exchange their interpretations of what had happened to them and who the casualties where during this hellish day of battle.

I knew we had lost Captain Andrew as I personally saw him fall with such bravery trying to rescue others when a bomb exploded in the hollow.

I overheard Private Atkins talking to others when he announced that Private Watson had been killed, by an explosion close to the wooded area.

I had been wondering where Jim was but I understood he had gone on a retriever job helping to collect the injured and identify those who had fallen.

I stopped Private Atkins in the middle of his conversation, with a trembled high pitched voice, to ask him are you 100% sure Private Watson is dead. "Yes," he said "I'm one hundred percent sure Alan is dead". As soon as he said Alan I was selfishly relieved that it was not Jim Watson, but sadly it was Private Alan Watson who I knew by sight only.

Initial headcount was devastating as we had heavy causalities of all ranks.

I also learned that we had lost a really good lad we met during a social event. He was a charming Yorkshire man from Bradford, a gunner with the Royal Artillery who had served in Sicily and was wounded but returned to duty.

I felt very sad to hear the news as he was 32 years old, so proud to be the father of six children, the eldest being 10 years old. I just cannot imagine how Mrs Crawford will handle the news, Luke was indeed a great soldier and a gentleman.

Our tanks had arrived giving a temporary cease to attacks from the Germans and ideal time to dig in for the night.

The enemy sent out patrols to ascertain our strength of defences with further light occasional shots being exchanged.

Daylight came with little rest, however Jim and I were able to catch up on the previous day and exchange our views with mixed feelings.

I told Jim that yesterday was the first day I thought I had no chance of survival, thought I would not get out of the field alive and that despite much loss of life I selfishly was glad we made it.

I can still hear the sound of our boys screaming from the shrapnel wounds ripping holes in their bodies and obliterating complete limbs.

Next morning orders were given to attempt to advance closer to Breville from the North side. We split into small groups some crossing by field in trench positions some edging the woodland approach and appeared to be making progress despite much sniper and mortaring in all areas. Then suddenly early afternoon we could hear enemy tanks moving on the north side and heavy enemy barrage descended on all positions.

I could see the shells exploding in the trees and shattering shrapnel all over the place and reaching our trenches even some direct hits into our only cover.

We managed to hold them at bay and we could see we were causing them problems as many Germans had fallen on the battlefields.

Still Gerry was knocking out our anti-tank guns they obliterated our Bren gun carriers leaving us basically with small arms and mortars, however, we knew we had given them a good kicking.

They hit us for maybe three hours constantly until suddenly things quietened down.

We waited and waited thinking they would start again but they did not, then we welcomed the arrival of the Canadian Para's, giving strength to the battalion. Time to regroup and assess the damage to casualties and equipment.

I had not seen Jim since noon, as he was away with the captain, less than 500 yards from my group but more on the woodland side.

Our boys were returning to base in dribs and drabs when I spotted Jim covered in blood, with a blackened face, his arms draped over the shoulders of two privates hardly able to walk.

I rushed to help and I could not believe the glazed look in Jim's eyes, he didn't even recognise me and was mumbling senselessly.

I could not identify where he had been hit as he was totally covered in blood and filthy mud, he remained gazing like a zombie. I guessed this was the end of the war for Jim.

He was then taken away to the field hospital by the two privates as I was told to stay put by the corporal. It was apparent that the Germans had not finished as their tanks were repositioning in preparation for a further attack.

Just by a near miracle we received a radio message to say HMS Arethusa was anchored offshore and was capable of hitting the German target given correct map references by shore-based Naval Forward Observation officers.

We cleared the area and Major Dunn gave the go ahead for gun zeroing to be taken.

Then suddenly the first naval attack took place, absolutely spot on target, killing loads of Germans and wrecking tanks with devastating effect.

Followed by a second blast, doing even more damage, leaving the remaining Germans to scramble away out of sight.

We were now in a safe position and able to take a well-earned rest.

My concern was for Jim but apparently we had so many casualties that no further news was available, I can only be grateful that he is still alive.

After a couple of hours I made contact with the two privates who had retrieved

Jim and they told me that he was the only man alive in a group of bodies and it looked like they had been hit just as they had gone for cover in a trench when shrapnel and bullets where dropping on our lads with incredible accuracy.

Corporal then told us that today we had lost more than 20 colleagues and there were maybe 100 wounded. A week ago 900 of us 5th Black Watch soldiers landed at Normandy and today we are down to 600 with 90 deaths and over 200 casualties.

It really made me think that if we can lose a third of our lads in a week how long will it be before it was my turn.

Also, I think about the older lads telling us recruits how wet behind the ears that we were and yet after one week it would be me telling a new recruit the same story.

In one week I have witnessed things too gruesome to articulate to anyone who has not experienced it themselves.

Following a meeting with 3rd Para Brigade our CO informed us that we were to attack Breville and the attack would be supported by field fire from medium Regiment Royal Artillery and we would be off at 10pm. that evening.

Knowing we had given Gerry a thrashing earlier, we were relatively confident that Breville would not be defended.

The CO was correct. After a fierce battle we took over Breville and captured the 346th German Infantry

Division with them suffering losses of both men and equipment. This was a significant achievement as it prevented them from mounting subsequent assaults on other Allied lines.

Early on Tuesday 13th June we were relieved by the Oxford and Buckingham Light Infantry as we marched to a rest area close to Le Mesnil.

We enjoyed a good meal and were told to have a good night's sleep as tomorrow we would hopefully spend the day formulating plans.

Next morning the CO explained that we had lost so many men on the approach to Breville and although some of the casualties were now fit for action, some of those injured had passed away. Also we were still well undermanned and that he would fill the needs and had made it clear upstairs that it was crucial we received reinforcements of both men and equipment.

He also took time to tell us how proud he was of us all in maintaining the honour of our regiment.

So nearing the end of a peaceful day, with everyone relatively relaxed, another tragedy happened. Our battalion area was bombed by our RAF killing four and injuring several of our lads, two more dying later. No explanation was given about this dreadful mistake only to say it was probably due to fluid battle situation throughout the Normandy Bridgehead. In other words: another serious cock-up in communications.

Later I talked to the medic who was called to the scene of the accident, and asked about Jim.

He told me he had no physical injuries other than cuts and bruising and the blood I saw was that of his colleagues, maybe he had tried to drag them to cover where they were found in the dugout, however, he was in a terrible mental state formally known as shell shock or more recently as battle fatigue.

He explained that in some cases the best treatment was to get the patient back into battle as soon as possible, however, in other cases it was going to be a lifetime of hell with nightmares and uncontrollable recurrences of the original triggered situation.

He said Jim would need to be returned to England where he would be treated at Bangour hospital in Edinburgh.

He also explained that there was a new treatment being tested by the hospital that included hypnosis and that there was a more sympathetic understanding of the illness and recovery to a normal life is on the increase.

He closed by saying, everyone had a breaking point, weak or strong, courageous or cowardly, this happens throughout all ranks and it is the commitment of medical staff to relieve the person of a possible lifetime of mental illness.

Before finally sleeping that night I was devastated to have lost my best friend and prayed I could get through this hell and see him again in Huddersfield, maybe watch Town play, and have a few beers.

At the same time I could not stop thinking about who was the lucky one.

On the 14th June we were based at 153 Battalion's HQ close to Le Mensil as we took a defensive position awaiting the arrival of reinforcements.

Later we were joined by Royal Scots from Aldershot and men from Normandy Reinforcement Camp. Officer replacements included two majors and a number of NCO's took place hopefully giving some depth to the battalion.

Padre Nicol with help from Ed Meckison returned to the Breville battle scene carrying a number of small wooden crosses in a hope that they could pay their respects to those who had given their lives now in temporary graves.

Despite being fired upon they continued the task in hand and eventually the firing stopped, maybe it was the enemy's way of sharing respect for the dead. We had a couple of days of reasonable peace until the Germans attacked at 4.30 a.m. along the whole front of the River Orne a fierce battle took place for a few hours and thanks to Derbyshire Yeomanry they managed to knock out four tanks and a couple of armoured cars and by lunchtime the Gordon's and Derbyshire had full control of Escoville.

Today we received the first issue of "P1obaireacha", strange name for the battalion's newsletter; something that would keep us informed what was going on throughout the war effort and gave chance for our superiors to motivate the troops. First issue read as follows.

"This is the first daily newssheet to be issued since the Division returned to France. Four years ago, our Division fought the Germans in France. Through weight of numbers, overpowering air support and equipment generally, the Germans were then able to oust us, despite every gallant endeavour, from France. Today the picture is different. The much vaunted Western Wall has been pierced and shattered by the assaulting troops. Already we have been into France, well into France too, for 9 days, whereas the Germans said they would defeat the invasion on the beaches. The Division has played its part, with at first only small forces engaged, in a notable way towards the 2nd Army's grand achievements. The 5th Black Watch, the first battalion of the Division into action, has covered itself with glory, and the fields of Normandy with dead Germans. The Gordon Highlanders have had a good fight, and have more than held their own. The Seaforth and Cameron Highlanders were in action, and ready as always to do likewise. Our Gunners, and Machine Gunners, have already fired many shells, bombs and bullets, had many successes and done much sterling work.

And so have all the other units in the Division.

So we have made a start. Not a spectacular start, such as was the Division's fortune at Alamein, but a brave start none the less. Before us lie hard days and hard fighting. But there is no doubt that our present operations are going well, and that we are making a great contribution to those operations.

Let us go ahead, then, with confidence in ourselves, faith in our cause and with a grim determination to do our best at all times, so that Germany can quickly be brought to her knees, and the War won.

To all ranks in the Division, I send you my greetings, and the best of good luck. I have absolute confidence in you. So has the Army.

In Africa and Sicily, we showed the world what the sons of Scotland can do. That was nine months ago. We will show it again now." (Signed) D.C. Bullen-Smith.

For the next few days similar attacks took place and on 19th June it poured down with rain and believe me, the last place you want to be under wet conditions is sat in a slit trench waiting for action.

Returning to base I was greeted by the corporal who, with a gentle, concerning voice, said "Got some news for you lad, Private Watson has arrived back in Edinburgh where he is being treated at Bangour Hospital, hope he gets better soon, and you must try to put last week behind you as you need a clear head and don't worry about Jim he is in good hands now."

Back on dry land, today I will write to Jim's parents and my Mum and Dad to let them know I am aware that Jim is in hospital and maybe get some news from them. For sure Jim's Dad will be heading for Edinburgh.

They will have no idea of the hell we have been through and to be honest I don't want them to know, I try and keep my letters brief and focussed on the happier events.

No sooner had I finished my letters when it was announced that the long-awaited post had arrived along with newspapers, looking forward to catching up this evening.

Some of the lads, despite the thick mud, had managed to acquire some potatoes and fresh vegetables from a nearby derelict garden, not that we were short of food but the variety was welcomed.

After a couple of days of relative quietness locally, on 21st June for the first time in 2 weeks, 153 Brigade were all together again as we had been split up moving from one command to another since landing in Normandy.

The atmosphere was very positive as the boys compared their experiences of the last couple of weeks.

Lots of camaraderie as we joked about things back home, Private Peacock announced his wife was pregnant only to get a reply "check your leave dates of 3 months ago". One guy said it was his wife's birthday and she loved diamonds so he said he would send her a pack of playing cards.

It is rumoured that after the breaking of Caen the allies will take over Paris within 3 weeks forcing Gerry on to his own territory, if correct maybe my war will be short lived.

We are also informed of a change of leadership and that Major Dunn was to take command of a composite force of our B and D company and 1st Gordon's, it's all too complicated for me so I will stick to doing as I am ordered.

Huns had been dropping propaganda leaflets that told us that they had obliterated most of the cities in Britain and that we should surrender.

Corporal told us to keep them as they would come in handy if toiletries were in short supply.

The next few days would give time for new arrivals to settle in and be updated on the battalion battle drills and forthcoming plans.

Marching to Beny-sur-Mer meeting up with 8th Canadian

IWM B6000 - Led by the Pipers, of 7th Seaforth Highlanders

IWM B5664 - 25-pounder field guns in action during an
attack on Tilly-sur-Seulles,

Tanks of the Royal Marines on their way to Tilly-sur-Seulles,

To be feared, German Snipers, at times virtually invisible

Obstacles to be feared, German land mines.

The fear of being hit, Canadian medics at work

The unforgettable site of those colleagues killed.

What the nation read on the headlines 23rd June

Our parents, friends and family would read the Yorkshire Post

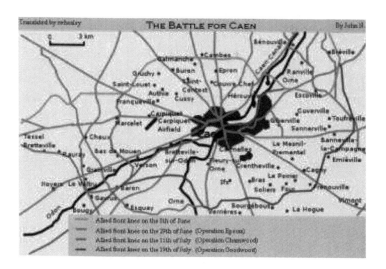

By the end of June we were holding our ground east of the River Orne.

From high ground from Ranville we could see the tall chimneys of a factory in Colombelles knowing it was being used as an observation post by the Germans. This was a prime spot for the enemy as our recce had experience their awareness of our presence and we had identified they were holding the sight with some strength.

It would be a few days before a decision on the attack of Colombelles would be made, meanwhile we were relieved by 5/7 Gordon's and took over a position further South of le Bas de Ranville.

On the 10th July the plan was to attack Colombelles that night and would be carried out by 153 Brigade plus 7th Black Watch, well supported by Sherman tanks, anti-tank gunners, a platoon of Middlesex machine gunners and a platoon from 276 Field Company Royal Engineers.

The 5th would approach from the North-East side of the factory and secure the crossroads while the 7th BW would occupy the factory area.

The Gordon's would secure the village.

Royal Engineers plan was to blow up the two chimneys.

It was estimated this would take 24 hours to complete. Everything was in place we all knew our orders, we were out of sight of the enemy, well dug in, all in readiness for the morning of 11th July when battle would commence.

News came that the Gordon's had been unable to secure the village of Colombelles and would need a second attempt early in the morning.

Until this was completed we were exposed on the right flank, therefore alternative plans were being made.

The attack on the village alerted the enemy as they began to counter attacked with great force. They began shelling, mortaring and lighting up the skies with flares.

From their observation posts they could detect every movement giving them a great advantage, we were now in a very serious situation.

Soon attacks were coming from three sides and it was clear we were suffering loss of life.

We attempted to dig in deeper but the ground was very hard so slit trenches did not offer adequate cover.

I could see that German tanks were closing in and blasting our Sherman tanks out of sight, it looked like none had survived.

Surely we are all going to be totally wiped out. There is no way we can defend ourselves without our Sherman's and anti-tanks.

As daylight appeared we were ordered to withdraw under cover of continuous smoke from Divisional Artillery making it to Ste Honorine two hours later.

Once temporarily secure, we could sense the friction amongst our leaders as harsh words were exchanged for all to hear. It would appear that we had totally underestimated how well the area was secured by the enemy.

The Germans had taken out 10 of our 11 Sherman tanks and an anti-tank and we had no idea how many men had survived or had been taken prisoner. All I know is that somehow I got back but I could see we had lost many and the morale and self-esteem was as low as it can get.

Later we got the soul-destroying news that the total of men killed, missing or taken prisoner was 128 including 5 officers.

In just 8 hours we had lost 25% of the fighting strength of those involved.

Word was getting around of the anger expressed by our leaders and recriminations and innuendoes from various ranks were rife causing much discomfort around the camp.

In conclusion, the divisional plan of attack of Colombelles was a shambles and we had been exposed to an impossible task and that any reflection on the fighting qualities of the Black Watch soldiers, as a result of the plan, would be grossly unfair. Later that night, fighting patrols returned to the battle scene in an effort to recover some of the kit but enemy presence prevented them succeeding.

They arrived back at 3a.m followed by shelling of our area causing more casualties, including Captain Turner and Lt. Phillips.

The next day a determined fighting patrol returned to the Colombelles fields and managed to recover most of the kit successfully.

This gave the battalion a few days to rest while the kit was being repaired.

We received an announcement that Padre Nicol was returning to the UK and would be replaced by Rev Ross.

Padre Nicol was well-liked and respected by all and in particular gave myself and Jim comfort after his shell shock incident in June.

By coincidence, today I received a letter from Jim from Edinburgh, it was just fantastic news and I must have read the letter ten times this evening.

Jim returned to Edinburgh and as planned he was taken to Bangour Hospital which was the designated hospital for most Scottish regiments.

He was being treated for his breakdown and told me the staff were brilliant, kind and understanding. His father Albert and his sisters, Alma and Jenny had been to visit him which gave him much strength and helped him to relax.

The doctors told Jim of their plans, he would stay in hospital for an initial recovery period and subject to his progress, he would be allowed some home leave. Their objectives, however, were to get him back to Perth Training Wing as soon as possible so they could assess his future potential.

Jim made it clear in his letter that he wanted to return to battle as he and the doctors thought it would be the best treatment to rid him of the demons in his head that had haunted him since that day in June.

I would have preferred him to stay in the UK and be safe knowing what the last few days have been like and to be honest, I wished I was home. I wished the war was over, this life was sometimes unbearable and sometimes hard to comprehend what the hell we were doing there.

Sunday 16th July I went to our first church service given by Padre Ross. He gave a wonderful talk about the way we should ask God for guidance and assurance while we are fighting for our loved ones at home.

This was followed by a great night out entertained by the Pipes and Drums during which some of the local French families joined us.

Bearing in mind the French had been invaded and under German control for 4 years, you can imagine how welcome they made us knowing peace for them was in sight.

We could now look forward to a few days rest before heading off to Ranville.

On arrival at Ranville we moved into some old farm buildings, the weather was dreadful with torrential rain, so bad it was enough for us to receive a rare ration of rum which went down a treat.

It was announced today that Lt Colonel Thomson was to return to the UK to take command of the 10th Black Watch and that Lt Colonel Bill Bradford would be taking over his post.

A farewell party was held for Colonel Thomson; another lively evening followed by Pipes and Drums.

The Lt Colonel gave a farewell speech the following

morning when he thanked us all for our support and asked us to continue to maintain the standards of the 5th and its great traditions also that we should give the same commitment to his successor.

A couple of days later Lt Colonel Bradford arrived and was welcomed with much sincerity, especially by the older lads who had knowledge of the man's history serving with the battalion. Immediately there was a change of atmosphere amongst the lads almost a celebration and a sense of relief.

A further announcement that Major General Bullen-Smith was to be replaced by Major General Tom Rennie again this was welcomed by everyone, firstly because Rennie was known by the senior lads of his leadership skills, especially in battle. Secondly, the feelings were that of relief of the departure of Bullen-Smith as he had taken the rap for our failures and loss of men at Collombelles.

Jim and I had met Rennie in England during our training when he gave a speech on the battles commencing at Alamein with such power and conviction that one immediately knew he was a man's man and one of us.

So that was something to look forward to in the coming days.

Today we had some further news on the progress made by the Allies, Caen had been taken by the British, the Americans had taken Cherbourg, Montgomery had ordered a drive towards the Seine and our Canadian friends would capture Falaise. This gave further confidence to us all that we were winning and it was only a matter of time and that maybe we will see less fighting and more clearing-up operations.

On 6th August we were moved by the Royal Army Service Corps troop carriers through Caen on our way to Cormelles where we would then march to Bourguebus to take over from the Argyll and Sutherland Highlanders of Canada.

Caen was an unbelievable sight to witness, the place was in ruins and something I will always remember.

From the day the Allies landed in Normandy, Caen was a key target as it was one of the largest cities it laid astride the River Orne and Caen Canal giving the Germans a strong defensive advantage if not crossed. Also Caen's road system would allow Allied forces to shift resources quickly.

The capture of Caen had proved more difficult than originally planned, however, the Allies including American, British and Canadians had done a good job. This was followed up by our Royal Engineers doing a clean-up job on mines and booby traps prior to our arrival.

We were told that the Germans had shot prisoners of war killing over 100 Canadians, when we have taken prisoners we have treated them with respect, fed them shared cigarettes from our own rations so to hear this kind of treatment it was easy to hate the Germans. The once wonderful cathedral was badly hit along with factories, the university and many homes leaving 35,000 French residents homeless.

After arrival in Bourguebus the town was also badly damaged and the Canadians had warned us of German sniper fire mainly at night time.

The CO read out a message from General Rennie explaining that the Highland Division was about to enter into a battle under the command of the 2nd Canadian Corps and this could prove to be the decisive battle in France.

It also said that the success of the battle will depend on the determination and offensive spirit of every person in the division and, finally, wished us all good luck.

We were moved out of town knowing that a further Allied air strike would take place shortly before midnight. The last two vehicles to leave were hit by bombers who had dropped on the outskirts of town but fortunately only wounding the guys that included our Medical Sergeant, however, they made it back to the battalion with minor injuries but totally shaken by the experience.

The next day we had orders to move to an assembly area on the Caen to Falaise road where we would patrol through the 1st Gordon's taking forward positions in front of the village of Sequeville la Champagne when the Gordon's were to take the village of La Hogue.

1st Gordon's reported that La Hogue was not held secure and that we must move in as soon as possible. Our attempt to enter the village was halted by the cratered roads and mines and this took a few hours to overcome.

The village had been flattened by the RAF earlier and we had little resistance when entering the site. We found a few Germans hiding in the ruined buildings but they surrendered without a struggle.

The battalion then took orders to move into St Sylvain where the Polish had not captured the village and required us to help them finish the job.

The Poles were short of rations yet most of them appeared to be under the influence of alcohol and were disorganised, lacking discipline and leadership. We were told by the Poles the enemy was mainly active and holding strong in a chateau close to the woodland.

Again the roads around the village were impassable, good work from the Royal Engineers as they bulldozed through the rubble.

We entered the village without any opposition. With no Germans in site, allowing us to move towards the chateau only to find it unoccupied.

The enemy counter attacked from a distance with mortars and artillery. We were ordered to take cover in the remains of the building. This continued throughout the night and we suffered minor casualties. The following day the shelling continued injuring Major Munro and Padre Ross slightly, we were put under command of 7th Argyll and Sutherland as they had taken a hammering with severe casualties.

On 14th August we were informed of our daylight

attack on the neighbouring village of La Bu Sur Rouves supported by two squadrons of tanks from 148 Royal Armoured Corps. Fighting started on arrival with several enemy machine-gun fire as well as intensive mortar fire.

We stalked the machine guns and managed to put them out of action killing most of the enemy and allowing the battalion to move forward giving support to the front liners. Thanks to the Canadians with their tank force we managed to capture the village and take 200 prisoners along with some useful kit including anti-tank guns and mortars.

Time now to count our losses of the day, which totalled 6 killed and 34 wounded, we then took time to reflect, relax and generally have a clean-up.

The next day, following a recce the battalion was called to the village of Percy en Auge. On entering with no resistance a Forward Observation Officer entered the church followed by an exploding booby-trap because of which he was killed outright.

That was the only incident of the day as the village was clear of any threat.

We spotted that there was fruit growing in the gardens, ripe peaches and pears for the taking. They were delicious and a first time experience for me actually picking a peach.

Our next move was to cross the bridge over the River Dives at Ouville, however, reconnaissance reported that the bridge had been blown up so we needed to make our way to another bridge 3 miles upstream. As we were ordered to move forward, followed by various vehicles, we encountered enemy fire we managed to knock out some German observation posts killing and taking a few prisoners.

We then came across a crowd of French refugees and escorting them to safe area of low ground, told them to stay under cover.

Most of the enemy were on the other side of the river bank still trying the odd snipe at us, but they appeared to be on the run.

A good days work as we had killed and taken lots of prisoners but sadly lost one of our guys and 3 wounded.

The brigade was to move to La Butte as the Gordon's moved towards Grandchamp. As we walked to the assembly area we were suffering constant attacks by our RAF and as darkness fell the Luftwaffe were dropping shrapnel bombs on us, fortunately we survived with only a few casualties.

You know it is really bad for morale when your own aircraft put you under fire despite us sending recognition signals.

On the way to La Butte we were told that the Gordon's had been successful in securing the bridgehead allowing vehicles to cross as soon as the pontoon bridge was constructed. They had suffered losses including Lt Colonel Hew Blair son of an officer who commanded in the Great War, he was well regarded by those who served under him. Despite capturing the bridgehead the Gordon's were still under heavy fire and as a result lost men including a few officers.

After only 12 weeks since landing in Normandy we have lost 168 of the 900 soldiers of the 5th Black Watch, hell knows how many injured.

Those killed represent almost 20% one in five killed in 12 weeks.

I learned today of the unbelievable action taken by some British soldiers who have only experienced 3 months of the war yet have decided to run away and hide. Their desertion of their duties something I cannot comprehend.

For sure they were not Black Watch boys. In fact I doubt they were Jocks: we stand together, fight together and if need be, die together.

Maybe continued shelling had sent them "bomb happy", a new term I've picked up for men doing strange things and acting crazy on shell shock. Let us hope Jim stays in England until this horrible war has ended.

Thinking about Jim I wondered if he would be home for the start of the new football season when Town are due to play Barnsley away.

The general situation for the battalion was made clear and the problems we were experiencing from the RAF continued.

Basically the German Army was undoubtedly retreating eastwardly, yet perhaps due to poor communication they were not retreating on mass, with lots of rear-guard actions and pockets of groups still counter-attacking as if confused.

It was difficult at this time to know exactly how our frontline troops were advancing again it was in pockets subject to the resistance they were getting. Therefore it was difficult for the RAF to spot how advanced we were as a battalion, we used yellow flares and large yellow silk squares to confirm to the RAF we were their Allies as these were not always seen we continuously shot up by our own lads from the sky.

General Rennie warned Air Operations if this continued we would have to retaliate with anti-aircraft guns available.

At the end of the day we move to take over from 5th/7th Gordon's who had been fighting in the town of Lisieux, on the way we were shelled and had sniper attacks and suffered another four deaths.

By the time we entered the town it was quiet. We took a rest in some of the buildings including a hotel. In the morning our objectives included clearing roads and the streets in the town left with many derelict vehicles and tanks.

Moving out of town to a rest area about 2 miles away the only site of the enemy was those Germans trying to surrender.

Good news, we are informed we are to take a couple of days relaxation.

Our CO had a note from the acting brigadier praising our actions as follows.

The two major attacks at Bretteville and Grandchamps (Le Butte) when you achieve the impossible are to my mind the two finest feats that the battalion has ever accomplished within my experience.

What a great signing off for the day, we are shattered, ready for a rest and hopefully a peaceful night, and to hear the words read out from the CO made me feel confident and reassured all was going to be OK; the Gerry is on the run.

The next day we were expecting reinforcements in the form of a large draft of new recruits out of training, plus some recruits from the affiliated battalion, the Tyneside and Scottish.

So for me it was a good night's sleep up bright and early tomorrow.

Early the next morning the day started with a good breakfast and lots of joking about with the lads and planning how we could initiate the newcomers. Strange that I was now be regarded as a veteran, one of the lads, a potential Jock, just 16 months after signing up.

After breakfast the new kids arrived looking immaculate with uniforms and kit straight from the quartermaster's store, the lads welcomed them like greeting a member of their family, the Jocks are very friendly, no edge, great lads to be alongside. I recognised a couple slightly older lads, as we had trained with them in Scotland, they were from Tyneside and Scottish who had landed at Sword Beach in June and had experienced the same traumas as we had.

Handshakes all round as we greeted the new arrivals and chatted with the Tyneside's about our experiences to date.

A voice from behind: "Na then Eric how's tha been". Could this be the voice I knew so well? As I slowly turned, I faced the man who had become like a brother. Hard to say you love someone, and, with Jocks around, forbidden to contemplate uttering the words. I needed to cry but just about controlled my emotions as I shook his hand and tapped the shoulder of James Watson, my mate Jim from Huddersfield, who was back in town.

Jim's arrival was perfect as we were having a rest period and could catch up on all the gossip. He looked so well, unbelievable after only a few weeks of rest and rehabilitation. Furthermore everything on the man was brand new, he looked like the rookies he had travelled with.

Wonder how Town will go on today at Barnsley said Jim, just like he had never been away.

Very soon after his arrival Jim wanted to tell me what had happened to him on that dreadful day and about his return to the UK.

He started by saying that when we were advancing into Breville he was with a same group including the captain, they were dug in at the edge of the woodland when the captain ordered that we attempt to head for the orchard giving us a strong position, just as we left the slit trench all hell let loose and shrapnel was flying all over the place ricocheting off the trees.

We were ordered to run for cover, back to the trench, me being the first to dive into the hollow, followed closely by three privates and finally the captain.

We piled into the trench as one soldier landed on top of me, as we laid in silence for what seemed to be minutes, there was no movement from the others.

I could still hear spasmodic explosions so I decided to stay, also knowing I had not got the strength to release myself from the bodies on top of me.

My colleagues lay silent as I could feel the blood leaking from their limp, blasted bodies, I could feel no pain so I assumed I was not hit.

I suppose it was at least an hour before I could hear English speaking voices, it was our lads doing a clearing up job as they began to lift the bodies out of the trench until one of them said, "This one is alive". From then on I must have blacked out as the next thing I remember I was in the hospital tent. The place was packed with injured soldiers as the medics worked tirelessly. I just thought: why am I here? I am OK.

My mind was all over the place as I couldn't comprehend what was happening to me.

After, I think around 20 of us were shipped back to the UK, then on to Edinburgh where the regiment had taken over the hospital in Bangour.

I was just ordered to rest for a day or two and to be honest I still did not know why I was there, it gave me a feeling that I was a coward, duty dodger, weakling when deep down I wanted to get back into battle. The staff were brilliant, kind, considerate, devoted people and treated me with the same compassion as the lads who were seriously injured.

I was soon to learn that my experience in the trench that day had caused a temporary mental breakdown something they used to call shell shock.

The main treatment consisted of just talking over and over again about the incident to the doctor, he told me that the best way to come to terms with your problem is to accept what happened and try to have positive thoughts as my mind was full of negatives.

My parents and sisters visited one weekend and that really boosted my confidence and reassurance that I was back to normal.

After ten days I was released to Perth Training Wing, back to where we started, where I joined in with new recruits training, I think they wanted to double check my physical condition which was as good as ever. It was strange queuing up for my new kit with the recruits because it reminded me that we met for the first time in that very same room.

I was allowed a few days at home in Birchencliffe before heading south to return to duty here in France travelling with the new guys.

The only question in my mind about Breville was a guilt feeling that the guys with me had died and yet I had survived and I wondered whether we were shielded purposely by the captain, who gave his life. This I will never know.

We talked about how things have changed from our simple lives in Yorkshire.

How Friday night was special having worked all week,

when we would look forward to watching football on Saturday or for me having a few beers and playing Rugby.

How a pint with the lads on a Friday night became one of the biggest events of our lives.

Training with the battalion was both physically and mentally-taxing but, it was in many ways unreal, almost like Cowboys and Indians.

Remember at the cinema watching a film where people were being blown up or shot, it never affected your inner feelings because it was not really happening and this is the same when in training, it was just pretend.

We had never seen anyone die, never been to a funeral and never seen anything but a bloody nose in the school playground or at a sports event.

During the landing at Normandy we saw bodies in the water and on the beaches, but again it did not register as we were trained to accept this situation and in a surreal way you accepted it.

In battle we have shot the enemy but this has been maybe 50 or 100 yards away, again it does not appear to be real, you point your gun and fire, you see a man drop to the ground but you are not sure it was your bullet that killed him as there was so much firing going on around you.

You don't witness the death or feel anything for the man as he was just a target, he was the enemy. You see the bodies of the enemy lying around and somehow accept that it is just one less German. When you see a dying or dead comrade it sinks in and you go through a process of acceptance. It starts with you poor bastard, then you think about how he's only young and how his loved ones will cope with it. If he is older you can't help but think maybe he has a wife and kids. Finally you're glad it's not you.

We are supposed to be trained to handle it but you cannot train everyone to accept it, maybe you can brainwash them to think it's part of war but how can anyone expect us to be normal when we return home. We made a promise to each other; the word was the war was almost over, so all we have to do is tread carefully, no heroism, just self-preservation, and soon we would be back in Yorkshire.

The next few days was quite relaxed we had time for games, a bit of sport, playing cards and chatting with our friends and new recruits.

On 27th August we received our orders to act as Brigade Advanced Guard to advance through Bourg Achard to clear what was left of the retreating stragglers then move on to capture Barneville-sur-Seine while the 5th/7th Gordon's were to capture Mauny.

Just before arrival at Barneville we were told it was clear of the enemy and that we should join the others to capture Mauny.

About half a mile away there was a long hold up until the sappers had cleared the way, at the same time they were picking up German prisoners without any resistance.

The area around the town was tactfully planted with mines that needed to lifted, making the area secure.

We were hanging about by a crossroad, under cover of an orchard, waiting for the troops to arrive thinking all was quiet, when, suddenly, we were being shelled by the enemy which injured a captain and despatch rider. It soon quietened down, the shelling stopped and we considered ourselves lucky to have escaped further losses.

Early evening, supported by a squadron of tanks we advanced towards a chateau that we believed was being held by the Germans.

Almost immediately the enemy hit us with everything they had, small arms and mortar fire giving us the impression we were about to experience a tough fight.

Thanks to our tanks, we were able to storm the chateau capturing around 20 prisoners and finding many more dead and injured.

At the same time we were welcomed by a group of refugees found in the cellars. They had been locked up for a long time and just seeing the relief on their faces was a great reward.

By this time we realised that we had about 20 casualties ourselves.

Before dark we were led to a safe area that had been cleared of mines and fallen trees, where the battalion could gather overnight.

Spasmodic shelling continued through the night yet in the morning our patrols found no sign of the enemy. Sad to learn that Major Mirrieless was killed, a gentleman veteran with eight years' service with the battalion and he had only arrived back the same time as Jim on 25th August.

The next morning plans were made to head to a secure area to observe the crossing of the River Seine. On the 31st we became temporarily non-operational, time to rest and clear up before moving on to St Valery-en-Caux: a place that will bring back many memories for the vets who were there in 1940. It is now being blatantly obvious that the Germans are retreating with much speed, we are hearing news how well Allied forces are doing ahead of us and we are only finding a few prisoners. Most of our time is spent clearing roads and celebrating with the free French, they are very hospitable and appreciative.

Actually it's a good feeling chatting up the locals especially the younger females as we are considered heroes, however, the language is difficult, and even if they do speak a little English they don't have a clue what we are talking about.

After a few tastings of the fabulous wine, something new to us, communications flow much easier and romantic feelings begin take over.

I would be tempted myself but I fear the results after Private Dobson managed to score, with a prostitute, in Caen a couple of weeks ago and is now complaining about problems down below. He is trying to keep it quiet having already broadcast it, but we all have a laugh when he can't keep his hands out of his pockets. We are transported by Service Corps to St Valery via Rouen.

Rouen was once a beautiful place as you could see the remains of many of the Gothic buildings.

The French themselves had destroyed the bridges entering the city to delay the advance of the Germans. Later two temporary bridges were constructed only to be bombed by the Allies.

Many civilian lives were lost, not just by the Germans but by allied bombing, heavy rain had flooded shelters, the cathedral St Romain had been burnt down and the locals had lost 10,000 homes in the last three months, about the same time as our arrival in France. Last week Rouen was liberated by the Canadians and they and the Americans immediately constructed a Bailey, which is a temporary metal bridge, allowing freedom of transport for men and supplies. We were able to travel through Rouen to Silleron just outside St Valery.

Even the most recent recruit knew of the importance of St Valery as the battalion had lost so many men in 1940 on their exit from France heading for the channel. Battling to the end with little resources, lack of equipment, ammunition and man force, they never gave up until the inevitable happened and this was still remembered by the French who recognised their gallantry, as they welcomed us with open arms, respect, admiration and gratitude.

We passed a few small cemeteries around the place with the graves of 1st Battalion that had been tenderly cared for by the local people, despite the invasions and disruption to their lives.

We met two French girls wearing skirts made from Cameron Tartan, kilts they had guarded and treasured during their years of occupation by the Germans. The local schoolmaster had kept some of the personal belongings of the buried soldiers since 1940 and handed them over with pride to Colonel Bradford.

We made HQ in a local chateau, it was badly damaged but still plenty of space left, there was a feeling of celebration as wine was flowing, brought by the locals and in the evening we were entertained by the Pipes and Drums.

Many locals joined the party and General Tom Rennie gave an amazing speech to close the celebrations.

Later we learned that it was at Montgomery's request that the Division should recapture St Valery and he had asked the Canadian Army commander to arrange this, it was no coincidence that we and the 5th Seaforth and 5th Cameron's were united on this day in memory of our colleagues, today 3rd September it was announced that it would be remembered as St Valery Day.

Morale was at a peak the lads were on a high we were all aware of the next move to Le Havre where the Germans were still holding out and the combined effort of the 49th and 51st would hopefully take La Havre, completing a major part of our objectives in France.

Since mid-June the British have been bombing La Harve the major port north of the River Seine which the Germans have occupied since 1940.

Our Lancasters, we believe, have destroyed key German bunkers and most of the City is in ruins, however, the Germans are still holding out. Thousands of residents have been evacuated to refugee camps in the British-zoned areas or farther afield to neighbouring towns and makeshift shelters during this period. Le Havre continues to operate through the messiness of war.

Our job is to liberate Le Havre, the final stronghold of the Germans and drive them back to their homeland territory.

The plan is for the 49th Division to attack from the east and the 51st Highlands to attack from the north a strongly defended coastline, however plans changed on route.

The planes are coming over in endless succession for about an hour literally pouring out bombs. I could actually see the bombs leaving the planes, it was a terrifying sight, but horribly fascinating. Meanwhile, there were showers of green and red explosions like fireworks lighting up the skies.

I hope they know we are down below this time.

The 49th Division started the attack at around 5pm and by 11pm they reported all was going well, we then moved with 5th Seaforths through the 49th positions moving westward to capture key positions, if possible before dawn.

The battalion advanced, following the Gordons to just outside Foret de Montgeon where we would attack the enemy gun positions.

We received a message to say our tanks and transport ahead had snarled-up as the minefields have not yet been cleared completely and the enemy was persistently shelling the gaps cleared.

It was evident that we were suffering casualties as the enemy shelling was very accurate. The CO, along with an Intelligence Officer, went forward to assist the clearing of the road through a wooded area. When the road was clear we advanced in sight of the enemy and were able to counter attack with great force, so much so that we could see a stream of Germans surrendering without further resistance.

Some local residents began to appear giving us information on the whereabouts of the enemy, some holding jugs of beers for our boys.

They even gave help in rounding up the prisoners. There must have been 40 or 50 Germans freely surrendering.

The enemy was still shelling from a convent that needed to taken and there was sniper fire from the church and surrounding buildings.

With determination and support from Crocodiles we capture the convent, taking more prisoners.

The snipers were operating from the church tower and pill-boxes, with a combined effort from the Battalion and help from our 6-pdr anti-tank gun, we managed to demolish the church tower and stopped all further sniping.

It now looks like we can enter the town centre with little problems. The immediate problem was to deal the prisoners now counting about a thousand.

A prisoner collection point was established by the wooded area to be processed where they would be sent a further two miles back to Divisional cages.

A corporal, along with six men and 15-cwt truck with a mounted machine-gun, escorted a batch of 500 prisoners across the countryside to the cages.

One could only smile when groups of local French came out from houses and barns, including old ladies armed with anything from broom handle to pitch forks as they insisted they helped the corporal escort the prisoners.

Whacking the prisoners in to line with sticks, they marched them down the road singing some French patriotic song.

One can imagine how they felt having been overtaken by the Germans for four years now in sight of a new future ahead, somehow it makes this life we are living all worthwhile.

The next morning 12th September we were ordered to take a clearing operation of the town Fort Tourneville, some fighting was still going on but only by retreating Germans and we were soon to learn that they had no further option but to scarper or surrender as prisoners. We were guided by the French to a local school which had been the HQ and billet of the enemy. It was intact but in a shambles, as the Germans had enjoyed a stock of Champagne and Brandy taken from the locals and this is probably the reason for the lack of fighting spirit they had left in them.

We were now able to take a rest, absolutely pampered by the French who showered us with small gifts of flowers and a welcomed drop of alcohol.

Time to recover as the battalion reassessed its stocks of vehicles as replacements were needed.

We have collected a whole host of German weapons again we can put to use.

The last few days we have lost another 16 of 5th Battalion comrades, including two friends who were killed, Bill Jones and John Rowatt. Jim and I will miss their company as they were two good lads, if it's of any consolation we have killed lots of Germans and collectively there must be thousands of prisoners. The CO congratulated us all on our endeavours and closed by saying

"Men, it is all over Le Havre is in the hands of the British"

On 13th September we received a message from the boss General Rennie.

The capture of Le Havre is another important task successfully accomplished by the Highland Division, this time in close corporation with the 49th Division. The casualties suffered by the Highland division were 13 Officers and 125 other ranks.

Our prisoners totalled 122 Officers and 4508 other ranks.

The number of enemy casualties is unknown, nor has it been possible even to estimate the number of weapons which have been captured in this heavy defended fortress.

The capture of the port of Le Havre should make a

difference to the future course operations and will speed up the final destruction of the German army.

The next day the battalion moved by transport to a small village called Beaurepaire, a quiet farming environment, the bonus was that we were all together in covered accommodation.

We were told we would stay for a further two weeks and it was unlikely we would have any attacks and that we would take advantage to upgrade our drills and weapon training ready to move on when called upon. We were given a 48-hour leave of duty but told we must keep away from the cities Paris, Rouen and Le Havre, as it was still a little dangerous. Some broke the rules and went to party in Paris but Jim and I stuck to the request and had a couple of quiet days.

Everywhere we went we were greeted by the appreciative French offering drinks and bunches of flowers, the girls were beauties also friendly.

In Perth Training Centre we had learnt a little French but not enough to get through, but somehow it did not matter.

Jim in his strong Yorkshire accent would say things like "mercy bucket". The French had no idea what he was saying, but they did understand, thank you. Life was full of parties when the massed Pipes and Drums would lay on the entertainment. Many of the celebrations were provided by the French who all of a sudden had found mountains of food, Champagne and Brandy.

The Entertainment National Service Association put on a brilliant show which included a guest visit by Gertrude Lawrence, who sang and danced, quite a glamorous lady even though she was in her late 40's. The guys just loved her.

We played sport including football as we watched the Incognitos beat 153 Brigade 11 goals to nil and then beat the 1st Gordon's 5 goals to nil.

The wireless also informed us that on Saturday, Town had beat Darlington 3-2 and Billy Price had scored two goals, what a result.

All in all a couple of weeks of sheer pleasure while still training and upgrading the kit in readiness. The reality of war returned today as we were told of our success in Le Havre and that the Americans would take over in an effort to get the port fully operational.

The Germans had destroyed much of the infrastructure while retreating and it was not until that today we learned of the extent of damage to Le Havre.

It is estimated that the town centre was completely destroyed during 5th/6th September by carpet bombing operations carried out by the Royal Air Force.

Meanwhile, the Germans, in order to prevent the Allies using the port facilities, before leaving destroyed 10 miles of quaysides. In Le Havre alone, 5,000 people were thought to have been killed, more than 12,000 buildings destroyed, 80,000 people left homeless and the remaining population had lost all tangible traces of its wonderful history. Today we had a beer with a

Frenchman Andre, he was helping the officers as a much-needed translator. He was a very interesting person, a member of the French Resistance and he told us of the goings on and how some Frenchmen had been collaborating with the Germans to gain favours. Some French girls had relationships with the enemy which was frowned upon by most people and if caught sometimes the French locals would shave off the girl's hair to show all what she had been doing.

Andre explained how the resistance communicated via radio to Britain. He went on the say:

"We didn't have a radio transmitter but our leader was in touch with a radio operator, and we got vital messages back from Britain through the BBC's radio broadcasts. The news was read in French three times per day, and the newsreader would always stop and say, 'Et voici quelques messages personnel', which means, here are some personal messages'. At first we thought these messages were from Free French in Britain trying to contact their families, but we soon found out that they were coded messages to the Resistance. Our radio operator was an amateur, and we were never sure that our messages had reached Britain until we heard the coded messages on the BBC. German vans with radio detection equipment using triangulation could pinpoint the exact location of a radio transmission within ten minutes, so my friends had to be very careful, if caught they would be shot. The radio operator who worked for us often moved location for his transmissions. In summer, when the corn was high, he would sometimes hide in a field while transmitting.

Of course the Germans knew that the BBC was transmitting coded messages, so they ordered everyone to hand in their radio sets. Many people hid their sets around the house, but for Resistance members this was too risky. I had a crystal set that was so small I could hide it in a bean can. It seemed an awfully long time between the beginning of May and 1 June, when the first message was finally broadcast, signalling that the invasion would happen within the next week. That Sunday, 4 June, I went to a party at a friend's house, as I stood there with people dancing all around me, I had this strange feeling that

I was like a little god, because I could see into the future.

I wanted to warn all my friends to go into hiding, but of course I couldn't say anything, not even to my parents, because I was sworn to secrecy. The next day, Monday 5 June, we knew that something would happen soon, because the train from Paris didn't reach Caen - the lines had been sabotaged. That evening I heard two messages - 'the dice are on the table', meaning we should sabotage railway lines; and 'it's hot in Suez', meaning we should attack telephone lines. My task that night was to watch the headquarters of the German 716th Infantry Division next door to our house, although I would have much preferred to carry out acts of sabotage. I was quite surprised that nothing happened at the headquarters until 3.30am. I had already met my mother on the stairs at 2am - she couldn't sleep because of all the planes going over, and the sound of bombing in the distance. Afterwards I learned that there were already about 20,000 Allied paratroops in Normandy at that time, but the headquarters only stirred into action at about 4.30am. At about 4.30am my mother was up again, saying that it had to be the landings. Of course I couldn't say yes or no, because I had been sworn to secrecy, but I told her perhaps we should fill some bottles with water. She also had the great idea to cook some potatoes and lucky she did that, because at 8am there was no more gas, water or electricity". These services were only restored again six months later

What a brave man, how interesting to hear his stories.

The Highland Division is now back to full strength and awaiting or next orders. In addition to our Squadron we have special units with their own specialist detachments, the Royal Artillery have long range field guns, anti-aircraft and anti-tank guns whereas the Royal Engineers would have men trained in laying   and   clearing mines, repairing and demolishing bridges, etc.

Then we have the back up from Medical, Transport, Supplies and Postal. The 153 Brigade has three infantry battalions, 1st, 5th, 7th Gordon's and we the 5th Black Watch.

We are then grouped into five units HQ, A, B, C and D companies and finally into groups of around twelve guys under the command of a junior officer or an N.C.O.

Sherman Tanks during an advance towards Caen

German soldiers guarding the factory in Collombelles

Happy days, time for a cup of tea and a rest

Everyone gets excited when the Postman arrives

We are so grateful to the Royal Army Medical Corps

Preparing wooden crosses for the temporary graves for
those who have fallen

Troops pick their way through rubble outside Caen

The ruins of Caen - July 1944

Caen Cathedral only just standing

A visit by Winston Churchill and Field Marshal
Montgomery in August

Local French people shave the head of a lady who had
Collaborated with the enemy

The French welcome 51 st Highlanders back to St Valerie-en- Caux

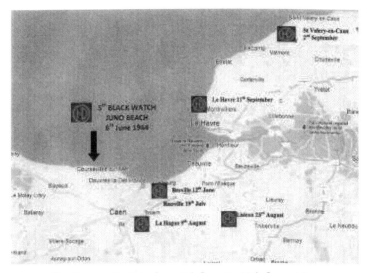

Our journey to date from 6th June to 11th September

What the papers say 11th September 1944

TO HOLLAND VIA BELGIUM

SEPTEMBER 1944

Today, 28th September, we have received details of our next move as troop carriers arrived to transport us to a Divisional Concentration Area near Ithegan North of Brussels in Belgium.

As we travelled north through France there was no resistance from the enemy as they had been forced to retreat by the sterling work from the Canadians, who had been moving north since their arrival in Normandy.

The Canadians were given the important tasks of clearing coastal areas in the north of France and capturing the launching sites of German rockets to put an end to their attacks on southern England.

The First Canadian Army also played a leading role in opening the Scheldt estuary, a tidal river and gateway to the Belgian port of Antwerp. Access to this port was essential to maintain supply lines to the Allied armies as they continued their push toward Germany to defeat Adolf Hitler's forces and free Western Europe from four years of Nazi occupation, which had begun in April 1940.

In most places it seemed the German's resistance

was faltering and Allied hopes were high for a speedy end to the war.

Travelling with the lads it gave time for boyish joking especially talk of sex, Andy started with saying; "sex is like a Rolls Royce, that's right, I don't have a Rolls Royce".

Followed by, "A joke is like sex, neither is any good if you don't get it".

McDonald came up with Confucius quotes.

Confucius said: "It's ok to let a fool kiss you, but don't let a kiss fool you."

Andy replies, "A kiss is just shopping upstairs for downstairs merchandise".

Smithson, one of the married men, piped in, "marriage is like a bank account, you put it in, you take it out, and after a while you lose interest".

"When my wife gives me the silent treatment, she thinks it's a punishment".

This went on for what seemed like hours, there is always a joker in the camp no matter how tough things are and you can rely on the Jocks to see the bright side of life. If they are not telling jokes they are taking the piss, and us Yorkshire lads are an easy target.

Our journey into Belgium at the end of September was a new experience as the battalion had relaxed, there was a great feeling of victory amongst the camps as we had partied during our travels northwards on route to Eindhoven. News that Brussels had been liberated on 4th September gave us confidence that a trouble-free journey was ahead of us and this was evident as we travelled through the towns and villages heading into Brussels. Monty had been welcomed by the mayor only a few days before our arrival and there was a great party atmosphere. The people everywhere gave us a great welcome, showering us with gifts of fruit, including peaches, grapes, tomatoes, apples and pears. People just cheering, where possible hugging and kissing the lads, and all ages were waving flags of black, yellow and red. Every building colourfully displaying their flags and streamers.

Having seen the devastation of Le Havre and Caen in France it was hard to comprehend how well Brussels had survived the bombings with little material damage.

The placed looked to be prospering as shops where open and the residents appeared to be clean, healthy and well-dressed compared to what we had seen earlier.

No doubt the German occupation for the past four years has caused indescribable misery and depression amongst the majority of the population.

The Belgian people have learned to hate the Germans as there is little doubt that memories of human suffering will remain for years to come.

Yet today their gratitude knows no bounds, maybe this is their way of demonstrating what is in their hearts. Our only disappointment was the fact that we were only travelling through as we would have loved to have stayed to party with some of the good-looking girls who outnumbered the local guys by at least four to one.

On route, 1st October, we billeted overnight in an old

mansion house in Hordain before moving on to take front line positions in Eindhoven.

It has been three weeks or so since we saw any action by the battalion, morale is still very high with no deaths since La Havre, we are feeling strong, well-fed and prepared for anything.

We are to take over from the 8th Royal Scots with an immediate task to hold the Nijmegen bridgehead still under attack from a determined enemy.

On arrival at St Oedenrode, doing day and night patrols, we were heavily shelled and most problems came from snipers, however, the enemy was outnumbered as we were able to retaliate with great force killing many of the retreating Germans.

Things soon quietened down overnight and as we welcomed a new day, one of the guys had shot a small pig and to our amusement he claimed he was a butcher by trade so we enjoyed extra rations of a pork lunch. In addition we discovered an empty farm house that had been occupied by the enemy which they had left hastily, leaving a barn full of chickens again supplying extra rations. A blind eye was turned towards the question of foraging as in this case it was not stealing as the barn had no occupants.

On returning with a dead chicken one Jock was informed by his staff officer: "Do you know you could be shot for stealing chickens?"

The jock replied "We mae git shot at any time so it makes nae difference"

Also in one of the barns we found a bitch with eight little puppies to the delight of the boys as we were able to put them in a safe place when returning to our rest area.

Very soon the locals began to appear knowing we had cleared the area of Germans and they showed great appreciation some of them spoke English as they were a mixed lot of French and Belgians, Flemish being the local language.

For the next few days we were split up taking time off in the rest area, where for the first time in ages we could take a hot bath, marvellous.

We may have been through hell but now it's playtime. We are in a good place enjoying a beer or two with female company and as one can imagine the locals are partying like its New Year's Eve every day. Jim received a letter from his father that included Huddersfield Examiner cuttings of Towns football results, Town had won 6 out of seven games played and Billy Price had scored 10 goals and Jimmy Glazzard 3 goals, a great start to the season.

We are aware and do appreciate the work of the Canadians who are ahead of us making life much easier as they are clearing the way to Antwerp which is a main supply route for the Allies.

The battalion will now move north to meet up with the Canadians forcing the enemy over the River Maas.

We are surrounded by criss-crossing rivers, canals and deep drainage ditches making it very difficult to move quickly, especially for our tanks and heavy vehicles and to make it worse it's been raining for two days. Training day today, we are to familiarise ourselves with Buffaloes which are tracked amphibious vehicles that can cross rivers and waterways.

We have new weaponry including Kangaroos which are tank type vehicles with Browning machine guns fitted, Wasps which are flame throwers, and Crocodiles which are flame-throwing tanks, much of theses we briefly saw during training in England.

Things must be getting safer as we learn that His Majesty the King had flown in to Zeelst airfield not far from us and the 154th Brigade had been given the task of protecting the airfield.

At midnight we advanced with the Gordon's to Wijbosh where we experienced heavy defensive attacks causing a few casualties, but we soon secured the area thanks to having tank support.

While taking a well-earned rest we could hear a strange squeaking sound coming down the lane on our right as we prepared to take cover then we caught site of an old man with a grey beard, flat cap, waving his hand while wobbling all over the place as he finally came to rest.

He then began to point back to the village shouting "German! German!" We gathered he was telling us that the enemy was active in the village about half a mile down the lane on the outskirts of Schijndel. We were then ordered to move on to the village and to be prepared for anything.

As we entered the village we were ordered to search every building for any remaining Germans and to be aware of snipers normally located in attics where they had perfect views of the streets.

Six of us entered a baker's shop that had been damaged with broken glass and debris all over the floor and stairs, Jim and I covered the doorway while the others searched each floor.

After a few minutes we spotted a solitary German tentatively walking down the street looking left and right in each building entrance with his rifle in a ready position.

We remained under cover of the shop doorway but watching his every move as he slowly got closer and closer to being able to spot us.

He came within ten yards of us as we both stepped out into the open and shouted at him to halt; he looked to be in panic as he made the mistake of raising his rifle and gave us no option but to open fire. We simultaneously fired one shot each hitting him in the chest area as he collapsed onto his knees yet still in an upright position his rifle skidding across the cobbles and out of reach.

The NCO screamed from inside the building for us to take cover so we entered the ground floor of the building and we could see the soldier through the window and he was still upright on his knees.

He only looked about 16 years old and he was mumbling in German "leider Mutter, leid Vater" which we believed to mean sorry mum and dad. He then rolled over onto his back and began to stamp his heels rapidly on the ground when the NCO took control by kindly finishing him off with a perfect shot to his temple. The well-experienced NCO knew of a trick that Jerry played by sending one soldier down a street in a hope that we would respond and expose ourselves for their snipers.

They have been known to take the uniform off a dead British soldier and play the same trick pretending to be injured and as one would naturally go to his help you would be shot down by hidden Snipers. I felt physically sick seeing that young boy suffer. If only he would have dropped his gun we would have taken him prisoner and he probably would have seen the war out.

I have shot lots of Germans, but always from a long distance when it did not mean anything, just one less German who was trying to kill us and you never really knew if it was your bullet that killed the enemy who would be 100 yards away and being fired at by many of us.

Today was the first time we had come face to face and killed someone, it is different when you can see what you have done and witness the pain and slow death of another teenager.

I will never forget that young boy on his knees with his eyes wide open gazing into open space and blood pouring from his chest creating a red stream across the cobbles into the gutter.

We continued to search the main street taking only

two prisoners believing the rest had scarpered to safety knowing we were on their trail and maybe finally accepting they were well beaten.

Returning to HQ that evening Jim and I had little to say about our experience both of us knowing what each was thinking, firstly that of guilt, then consolation as the German had raised his rifle to shoot us, then you think why are we here what has led us to kill each other, what good will come out of this bloody, terrifying, useless war.

Sometimes when you are on low ebb like now, someone will always do something or say something to totally change the mood.

Just as I am sat having a smoke, licking my wounds, Private Henry comes up with a poem he had picked up.

When there ain't no gal to kiss you,
And the postman seems to miss you,
And the fags have skipped an issue,
Carry on.
When you've got an empty belly,
And the bulley's rotten smelly,
And you're shivering like a jelly,
Carry on.
When the Boche has done your chum in,
And the sergeant's done the rum in,
And there ain't no rations comin',
Carry on.
When the world is red and reeking,
And the shrapnel shells are shrieking,

And your blood is slowly leaking,
Carry on.
When the broken battered trenches,
Are like the bloody butchers' benches,
And the air is thick with stenches,
Carry on.
Though your pals are pale and wan,
And the hope of life is gone,
Carry on.
For to do more than you can,
Is to be a British man, Not a rotten 'also ran,'
Carry on...

In the early hours of 24rd October Operation Colin began. Our objective was to take the town of Schijndel.

During the night the Gordon's would lead a silent attack from Eerde to Wijbosch, a village on the outskirts of Schijndel and we would pass through on the east side of the town.

Our day started with a wonderful moonlit sky and as dawn broke we commenced the advance across the muddy fields towards the town.

The leaves had fallen from the trees which gave us good vision but at the same time gave us little camouflage.

There was little opposition although the odd shell fell in sight of us but none or little machine gun fire was evident.

The Engineers had gone ahead of us to clear the

roads of mines so we assumed they were the immediate target of the enemy, they were alone and under fire but only from retreating Germans.

A group made an observation post from the top of a windmill giving clearance to advance led by "A" Company tanks.

Our first target was a large factory which dominated the town however the enemy had already scarpered with no resistance and we discovered it was only a silk stocking factory.

We were finding it difficult to advance as some tanks were having problems en route due to the muddy conditions when we heard from the Engineers that they had been heavily attacked and suffered casualties.

As we reach the town we unleashed a ferocious artillery barrage allowing us to advance with speed, the fleeing Germans had little further to offer as we could see them running away, some using civilian transport.

Shortly after taking the town, amid the blazing ruins the beleaguered locals began to appear from all directions. This was just how one would imagine an old Dutch town to be with old ladies wearing clogs and laced headdresses as they welcomed us with such joy.

The people had experienced the death of relatives yet managed to rejoice and celebrate our arrival.

They then produce a group of American airmen, who had been shot down, they had been hiding them from the Germans for several weeks knowing they would have been shot themselves for helping the enemy.

The Germans were never loath to torture when it suited them. What these people have suffered will be with them forever, their hatred of the Germans is clearly understood.

With Schijndel secured, 154 Brigade prepared to pass through 153 Brigade.

The 7th Black Watch mounted on troop-carrying Kangaroos, with the tanks of the 33rd Armoured Brigade in support.

The battalion moved on to the outskirts of the village of Esch were we set up a Concentrated Area. The bridge over the River Dommel had been blown up, however the Gordon's had crossed using a small foot bridge and managed to secure a bridgehead. Meanwhile the RE's had requested components to build a Class 9 bridge strong enough to take the weight of carriers and tanks to enable the attack on Esch.

We crossed the foot bridge and joined the Gordon's to give strength to the bridgehead, still experiencing some opposition by the enemy.

The Sappers building the bridge had suffered casualties but persevered with their normal determination and soon the bridge was complete. The 7th Armoured tanks were able to cross the river, but as we approached Esch all hell let loose with attacks from the enemy with Moaning Minnie's (mortar fire) as we suffered casualties during a stiff battle.

Company Sergeant Major William Latto of "A" Company was sadly killed.

We were killing Germans in great numbers, many of them surrendering as we took prisoners.

The tanks had set fire to some buildings on the way in killing many of the trapped enemy.

Jim and I were feeling the strain having had little sleep and every day seemed to be fighting days and the fact that in the last 3 days we have lost many of our boys including seven mates from the 5th Black Watch.

I think over the last few days we have had the worst mortaring since France in June and no matter what, you will never get used to the sight of dead comrades. We managed to take a rest, have some bully and vegetables and await the orders to move on to Loon Op Zand the next morning.

We also heard that Huddersfield Town had only managed a draw with Bradford Park Avenue having played them twice in a week but somehow it seemed irrelevant having had a bad few days in heavy battles. The next day we travelled to Loon Op Zand, experiencing enemy attacks from the pine wooded areas on each side of the roads, there was much confusion as it would appear that we had entered the enemy front line. The Germans managed to infiltrate right through the centre of the battalion splitting us up. We appeared to be fighting for hours before the tanks behind us managed to clear the enemy enough for us to be together and prepare a final assault.

Despite heavy fighting we managed to capture the village, yet still through the night the enemy was shelling and snipers firing at any sign of movement. For sure we had broken down the front line and taking lots of prisoners as the enemy was again in retreat leaving behind some important armoury.

Overall, it had been a good start to Operation Colin as all objectives had been achieved, casualties had been heavy but more than two hundred prisoners had been taken. However, we were told by intelligence that the German 59th Division had recently been reinforced by freshly trained paratroops and they remain a serious threat when we intend to approach our next target Hertogenbosh and cross the River Maas.

Our NOC, we called brain box behind his back, always insisted on letting us working class Yorkshire lads know how well cultured he was having had a superior education and was an expert on subjects like history , geography and what we like to call bullshit. He explained in detail that Hertogenbosch means "Dukes wood" as he pronounced it "bois du duc". It is an attractive old fortress town dating back to the Middle Ages partly surrounded by a moat he said as if he was a local.

Until recently the town was being held by the S.S. but heavy bombing by the Allies has probably persuaded them to find a safer location. Ok, to us it's just another town, another job, another day at the office so to speak.

The Royal Welsh Fusiliers had gone ahead to attack Hertogenbosch on 31st October and had reported that they had successfully driven away the enemy, taken many prisoners yet expected the Germans would regroup and be ready for us when we attempt to cross the river.

We entered the town to take over from the Welsh and it was clear they had done an excellent job making the hand over as smooth as possible.

The town was made up of little islands, a bit like Venice, but due to the Germans blowing up the bridges it made life difficult to get around.

We set up HQ on one of the islands able to take a rest with everyone coping well as we had a relatively easy arrival.

It was around 2 am when we were checking out buildings to clear any German stragglers,

We entered the grounds of a small farm house that was showing a glitter of candle light from the kitchen area.

Jim and I crept through a small vegetable patch, hopefully to get a view of the partly lit room. Through a small gap in the curtains we could see a lady preparing food at the long kitchen table.

We quickly checked the other ground floor rooms and there was no sight of activity, so we were satisfied the house was not occupied by the enemy.

Jim knocked gently on the kitchen door as I peered through the gap in the curtains I could see the feared look on the lady's face as she stood in hesitation. I called Jim to knock again and this time the lady responded and came to the door and partially opened it peeping out and with a quiet voice asked what we wanted bearing in mind it was the early hours of the morning.

Jim spoke quietly and informed the lady we were British and she should have no concerns as we would not harm her, despite understanding what we were saying the lady replied in Dutch hoping we would go away.

Jim then said that we wanted to search the out building as there were maybe Germans still in the location.

The lady relaxed slightly and in English said, "If you are English whereabouts in England are you from?" Jim replied "Yorkshire", she then said "Whereabouts in Yorkshire?" Jim replied "Huddersfield". The face of the lady changed completely and in perfect English she invited us inside the house.

"Would you like a cup of tea, are you hungry?" she asked as she filled a large kettle before placing it on the stove.

She then called out for her family to join us saying come down all is clear.

Within minutes her husband and two daughters entered the room greeting us like family.

The lady, Mable as we now knew her, explained in detail why she was so reluctant to greet us earlier.

Firstly she surprised us by saying she was from Wakefield in Yorkshire and that she had married a Dutch man and move to Holland in 1938.

She then went on to tell us that the retreating Germans were full of dirty tricks and determined to execute anyone from the Dutch resistance or anyone who were likely to give the Allies information of their whereabouts.

Mable told us that the Germans would even pretend to be English in a hope that we would speak freely and give them information.

There were still many families risking their lives by hiding refuges and in particular Jewish residents.

Initially, two years ago, reluctantly, Jews had to wear the Star of David on their clothing and those Jews eventually disappeared, either slaughtered or sent to concentration camps. Some ordinary Dutch people vanished for no known reason maybe for distributing leaflets or just upsetting the Gestapo.

Mable told us they are now experiencing the worst winter for many years yet we have no gas or electricity only the stove in the kitchen and food is so difficult to obtain.

"It is illegal to listen to the radio, if caught you would be sent to the concentration camps, however this does not stop us as my husband meets his friends to listen in to Orange and BBC radio in a hidden location." The family showed appreciation, they were a very gentle and softly spoken despite having experienced the trauma's, hunger and fear of the German occupation for a few years

Listening to that lovely family just reinforces why we had to go to war and how lucky our families are not being subjected to such horrors.

On leaving we told them to tell their friends we are driving the Germans out and that very soon the Netherlands would be liberated and free to build normal lives again.

Mabel with tears in her eyes hugged us both and wished us a safe journey and hoped we would soon return to our loved ones in Yorkshire.

We both had a feeling of pride as we returned to join the other guys dying to tell them about meeting the bonnie Yorkshire lass.

Our next big problem was how to advance to the River Maas when all the bridges had gone, how on earth are we going to get the vehicles across the canals? The surrounding countryside is very flat and prone to flooding the canals are quite wide but the biggest obstacle is the height of the banks making it virtually impossible to cross.

Recces have confirmed that the Germans are well dug in on the north side with clear vision making it too dangerous for the RE's to consider building bridges. The battalion therefore have to cross the canals securing a bridgehead allowing RE's to build in readiness for troops and armour to cross later.

It was decided that rafting the vehicles was the only way forward as we commenced practising using canvas sided assault boats at two points.

Later that evening the carrier platoon transported some boats to the banks of the Wilhelmina canal and assembled them ready for action tomorrow, however, when they arrived with a second delivery they discover that a Germans raiding party had managed to sabotage the boats, as they had crossed by rubber dinghy's under cover.

It would now take some time for replacements to be delivered.

On Sunday 4th November the CO gave out the plan of action he made it sound simple on paper but we were aware the enemy was watching our every move. So the plan was for C Company to cross on the right side, A Company on the left supported by with anti-tank guns and D Company would carry the boats over the banks, launch them and ferry 16 men each trip in a zig-zag motion across the canal. The Royal Artillery and the Middlesex Machine guns to keep the Germans busy while we attempted the crossing.

Jim and I were bloody freezing, it was so cold we were stiffened and we didn't fancy the idea of being in water. Anyway we climbed the banks to see a couple of boats had set off as we scrambled into ours, just as we were about to launch, the first boat ahead of us was hit by a bazooka fire and the passengers thrown into the freezing canal causing several casualties.

Not much we could do as there was no chance of turning back, I must say our boatman was brilliant. He fearlessly crossed the canal knowing he then had to go back to pick up more men.

We were ordered to scramble up the bank with speed and see those bloody Germans off otherwise our lads would be sitting ducks and any survivors from the hit boat would need to be rescued.

Around 30 of us took the Germans on with rapid fire and luckily they didn't fancy a fight and made it obvious they wanted to surrender.

Whilst climbing the canal bank we had no idea what

was before us, it could have been a disaster but this time luck was on our side.

Our actions allowed the others to cross safely, including Major Pilcher who congratulated us on our efforts.

We then went forward following the remaining Germans into a wooded area where they again gave themselves up without a fight.

With the far bank now in our hands, the boatmen having done a great job, we could see the arrival of anti-tank guns, jeeps and vehicles in support ready for the next move. News came that the Gordon's had successfully crossed the canal and transport would now be provided to move us to Haarsteeg.

During a rest period we were talking to some lads from 1st Black Watch and Cameron's who during the preparation for the crossing had been transported via Vught to Helvoirt. They had terrifying stories to tell about their visit when passing through Vught.

Working with 4th Canadian Division they entered Vught to find a group of Germans firing as they retreated into some woodland, after the Germans had made their getaway they found a large camp surrounded with high barbed-wire fencing. On entering the camp they discovered it was a concentration camp run by the SS who had made a swift exit unable to cover up what they had hastily left behind. In fact the first sight was two inmates hanging from some gallows, a site that terrified the young Cameron's and Canadians.

Then entering the courtyard they discovered around

500 bodies lying naked in a pile, possibly only executed that morning.

Most of the living inmates had run away from the camp knowing that the Germans had left in a hurry, many had nowhere to go so they started to return once they knew the camp had been liberated. These were the lucky ones as they would have been executed had the Germans had time to do so.

The people were in the most horrendous condition, starving to death, ill, and very badly mistreated.

The English-speaking inmates had plenty to tell our boys about the camp, it was divided into two sections, the first one was designed to hold the Jewish prisoners before their transit to German extermination camps. The pending Jewish prisoners didn't know that Vught was just a waiting room before their extermination.

The second section of Vught was designed as a security camp this section received all the Dutch and Belgian political prisoners, men and women.

The Germans were known to escort Dutch Resistance guys into the local woods, line them up and shoot them.

The guards were exclusively SS. the food was almost non-existent, warm water with some carrots or sauerkraut floating on the surface.

The SS guards tortured the prisoners with incredible cruelty, beating them to death. Several prisoners were brutalized with clubs wrapped with barbed wire.

The SS often provoked their dogs to attack prisoners

and there are several testimonies of horrible wounds, including raging dog attacks on various parts of the body including genitals.

Conditions in Vught were deplorable, hundreds of prisoners died as a result of maltreatment, shortage of clothing, lack of food, polluted water and various infectious diseases that were rampant in the overcrowded barracks.

The Jocks had left Vught in the hands of the Canadians who would sort the place out and try and bring some kind of normality to the lives of the inmates.

Some 30,000 people had passed through the camp in the last 2 years.

In conclusion, the lads from the Black Watch don't take pleasure from killing the Germans sometimes it is hard to justify, particularly when in close face to face combat.

Having heard these terrible accounts it somehow motivates or even makes you want to kill as many Germans as possible and that we should do so without any feeling of guilt or remorse.

It was announced that we would move out around midnight and head for Haarsteeg along with all companies, A, B, C, D, and join up with 1st Gordon's.

The RE's had almost completed the bridge that would enable heavy transport to cross. Some of the lads stayed behind to guard them and the bridge to catch up with us later.

We arrived to take up a safe position outside Haarsteeg without any problems, set up HQ and took up defensive positions.

We were reminded it was bonfire night tomorrow but this was one night we could do without fireworks.

During the night we could hear the arrival of S Company and the Pioneer Platoon, they had stayed behind to dismantle and transport our assault boats ready for our next crossing.

On route they were attacked by pockets of the enemy but managed to clear them off, killing some and at the same time taking more prisoners.

The last few days we had taken more than 100 prisoners and a collection of useful equipment.

We had a relatively quiet 5th November as we awaited news from a Recce party of 1/5th Queens Regiment, they reported that some civilians had given news of some activity from the enemy in a small village on the River Maas.

A small group of us went to investigate, but on arrival there was no enemy in sight, on our return we did see across the river some Germans we managed to fire possibly killing a few but the rest went into hiding, it was clear they were just a few SS stragglers. We decided to return to the village to make sure the locals were safe, by this time word had got around as groups of locals gathered to welcome us with the normal hospitalities and they assured us the enemy had left a few hours before our arrival.

The next orders were that we would return to Helvoirt.

The 5th Cameron's reported that they suffered heavy

mortaring when advancing through Heusden, about 5 miles away, they had heard a tremendous explosion ahead, on arrival they came across the burned and bombed remains of what looked like a church. Sixty women and seventy-four children died when the Nazis blew up the town hall in which they were sheltering. Before the detonation, the Germans had excavated underneath the bell-tower to ensure that it would fall on top of the terrified civilians. The SS had herded women and children into that building then they blew it up.

The next building to be liberated was being held by men in the black uniform of the SS.

The Cameron's closed in on them, giving them little chance to surrender and preferred to continue the attack by shooting the lot of them without a second thought. When you have witnessed the treatment the SS dished out to innocent civilians, women and children it makes the decision to shoot them on sight much easier to justify. Although we would not line them up and shoot them we would continue to fight even when we knew maybe they wanted to surrender. From that day on, any German wearing the black SS uniform would rarely get the option of surrendering.

The best SS man is a dead one.

We arrived back in Helvoirt midday on 6th November and we were allocated very acceptable billets allowing us to clean up and rest in comfort for the rest of the day.

The following day Pipes and Drums entertained the

lads as we were joined by other Companies and some civilians, it felt great to relax, chat with some new lads and exchange our experiences.

We were informed that we would move on to Leende tomorrow and that we should expect a trouble free drive as reports from the Welsh Fusiliers told us there was no sign of the enemy.

Still very cold and wet with occasional hailstorms and a definite threat of heavy snowfall.

An early start today as we were transported to Leende arriving at lunchtime. To the joy of everyone there was a Hot Bath Unit with open air showers and despite the cold we relished in the idea of a good soak removing some of the dirt and grime gathered over what appeared to be about three weeks' worth. Looking prim and proper we took up the offer of a drive by Liberty Trucks in to Eindhoven town centre. Nice place with some factories flattened to the ground, but generally looking tidy, the locals were friendly and there was a good feel to the place.

As a treat around ten of us decided to have a sit down meal and a few beers in a small restaurant almost taking over the place apart from a few locals. The waiter made it clear that he was short of cigarettes and was happy to wine and dine us if we wanted to barter, we got a good deal as the beer flowed like water although the food was basic.

After a few beers one of the Jocks headed to the corner of the bar where there was an old upright piano, with a confident look he seated himself down and started to rattle out some old favourites, to our surprise the locals knew the words in English and a good old sing song commenced bringing even more people in from outside, the place was packed with a great atmosphere so it's party time again.

Just as the place was buzzing a Corporal entered the place shouting out that the last chance to get back to HQ was parked outside and if we didn't come now we would have to find our own way back.

We had got carried away but you can forget about the bad times after a few beers. So we gulped our final beers down and rushed out to the street just in time to hop on the transport.

Requests came for a couple of pee stops on the way home and we were told to try to hide the fact that we were well oiled on return to camp.

The next day things quickly got back to normal as we were briefed to expect tough times ahead.

The day started with a message from our Divisional Commander, Major Tom Rennie read out by the CO as follows.

We of the Highland Division, with the 33rd Armoured Brigade and those units who have been working with us, can look back with satisfaction on the successful operations just completed.

During the period 23rd October to 7th November the Division, by its thrust from Schijindel to Geertruidenberg and its activities East and North of Hertogenbosch, cleared an area of some 300 square miles of Holland, denied Germans their bridge escape route at Geertruidenberg and captured or annihilated most of the Germans rearguards South of the River Maas.

The operations included the assault crossing of two rivers, the forcing of the narrow causeway from Waspik to Geerruidenberg and the assault crossing of the Afrwaterings Canal.

The success of the operations was due to the offensive spirit and troops and to the successful co-ordination of all arms.

The casualties of the Division during this period amounted to 44 Officers and 630 Other Ranks of whom 7 Officers and 115Other Ranks were killed. Prisoners captured amounted to a total of 30 Officers and 2,378 other ranks and casualties must have been very heavy.

The Commander of the 2nd Army, General Dempsey, writes of these operations

"Now that you have entirely cleared the country south of the River Maas, I want to tell you how greatly I appreciate the splendid way in which your Division has fought during recent operations. You had a great many difficulties to contend with, you overcame them in all the best possible way.

Please give the Division my very sincere congratulations"

We will undoubtedly have some heavy fighting to contend with before the war is won and we shall encounter better troops than those we have seen lately. It is the duty of every one of us to ensure that the fighting spirit of the Highland Division remains second to none.

The Germans had a strong hold and were giving the Americans a hard time around Weert, Roermond and Venlo.

Our next task was to cross the canals driving the enemy eastward, however, the canals and various ditches gave the Germans a very strong attacking position.

We needed to cross the canals using collapsible canvas boats, most of us had experience of them and we were aware how easy it was to capsize them. In preparation we practiced assembling the boats, trying them out on a local canal.

The most difficult part being loading and unloading quickly and efficiently. Being aware how exposed we will be to the enemy whilst crossing.

It was important that we had to drive the enemy away from the canals allowing RE's to assemble Bailey Bridges for heavy weight vehicles to cross.

Not the most pleasurable work having had a heavy social the day before.

We appeared to be well rehearsed and briefed as we moved forward to take over positions from the Welsh Fusiliers in the Leuken-Weert area. It was very cold and wet some of the lads had the cover of buildings but we were sent to a wooded area close to the Wessen Canal.

We patrolled the immediate area that evening but had no contact with the enemy so we returned feeling quite safe, however during the night, whilst taking a rest, a small group of Germans had crossed the canal and made a surprise attack on us. We managed to fend them off killing at least one of them and one of our lads was hit but only wounded.

This made us aware that the enemy was close and active, maybe just waiting for the attempted canal crossing. They made us feel edgy by having the tenacity to invade our patch just as final plans were in place.

Our plan was that 152 Brigade would cross the Noorder Canal the 154 Brigade would capture the lock gates at the junction of Noorder and Wessen canals. Our job was to cross the Wessen in boats clearing the way for Buffaloes to ferry jeeps and anti-tank guns. During the crossing we would be supported by artillery, mortars, tanks and Crocodiles.

Sappers would need to blow the banks of the canals to allow Buffaloes to negotiate the steep banks. So operation Ascot also known as the Battle of the Canals was about to commence.

Late in the afternoon we set off supported by Buffaloes carrying jeeps and anti-tank guns, flame-throwing Crocodiles and the Middlesex machine-gunners.

We could see that the crossing by the 5/7th Gordon's on the left was successful, no serious resistance was met and all objectives were secured as we took orders to go forward. The Buffaloes failed to climb the banks and had to abandon the idea of transporting other vehicles and arms.

The 1st Gordons simultaneous crossing on the right flank was much more difficult as a result of long-range mortar bombs landing on B and C companies suffering lots of casualties.

We, the lucky ones, managed to cross without difficulty although it was midnight when we secured our positions.

The Sappers were busy building a bridge across the Wessen to allow all transport to join us in the early hours, they arrived around 5 a.m. giving us time to take cover in some buildings and try and catch up with some well-earned sleep.

On the 16th November came a Warning Notice for an attack crossing another canal known as Uitwaterings in the vicinity of the Zig Canal.

The Gordon's would capture Roggell and we were to pass through ready for the next phase.

The canal was narrow, deep, and steep-sided and lay across the entire front and was assumed to be the enemy's main defensive line.

The attack would be led by 152 Brigade on the left, where the Zig joins the Noorder, followed by 153 standing by ready to exploit the situation.

Patrols reported that there was enemy movement and small-arms fire coming from the junction of the two canals and that the bridge there had been blown up. Early on 17 November, a heavy barrage pummelled the bridge area.

The leading platoon charged over the collapsed

bridge and took up defensive positions. We then followed their route and were able to meet up to quickly form a bridgehead. The enemy quickly became aware of the threat that this caused them and began to hit us with everything, intense bazooka, shell and mortar just raining down on us.

We just had to hold them back from the bridgehead, knowing reinforcements were imminent, giving them all the firepower we had.

Soon we had strong reinforcements, yet the Germans kept hammering us for at least 2 hours until a thick smokescreen counter attack was launched.

The Huns were not for giving in as they closed in on the bridgehead until our field and medium artillery hammered the attackers.

We were able to hold our ground but it was not until 1 am when the Germans finally retreated to safety. This was probably the worst fighting we had seen since France. The German observation posts were well sighted on the far banks of the canal and we suffered heavy casualties.

In addition to the German attacks, we suffered the consequences of that horrible anti-personnel mine known as the Schu-mine, named maybe because it was presented in a shoe box like wooden box. All around is soft muddy ground and these mines can be hidden so easily they can look like a brick or stone, they cannot be detected due to the wooden box They are capable of killing a victim, apart from the fact that even if you survive you will probably have lost limbs. They were scattered around indiscriminately and caused many injuries to the lads and were capable of putting vehicles out of action.

Torrential rain slowed the advance across the Zig Canal as our Flail tanks were stuck in the mud. A mine flail is a vehicle-mounted device made of heavy suspended chains with steel balls, like a farm implement that ploughs through the fields deliberately detonating mines in front of the vehicle that carries it, making a safer path for others to follow.

The carriers bringing our assault boats also got bogged down, and our sappers were working hard to clear the path and the road to the canal.

We had to drag the boats for half a mile across the muddy fields, under fire, some making contact with Schu-Mines until finally we reached the canal edge.

Around midnight we managed to cross the canal and secure the far bank. We were hit by German patrols yet after a strong battle against snipers we could see our lads were crossing almost trouble free. We lost some of our boys including a Canadian Commander Lt. Bill Cowan.

We later learned that some had fared much worse as a complete platoon was lost and taken prisoner and heavy casualties were sustained during the shelling. Jim and I were absolutely exhausted having had 72 hours of heavy rain, working through the night trekking across muddy plains under fire and in fear of those Schu-Mines.

The next morning brought good news as we were told that we would be transported back to Roggell and Heythuijen to take a rest, get cleaned up and hopefully get some dry clothing.

The facilities at Roggell are basic but at least we will be under cover and out of danger.

The next couple of days we managed to recover, both of us feeling well rested.

C Company had taken over a barn and turned it into a temporary theatre to give us all a great concert, followed by a farewell party given by the Officers for Major Wright who had a new posting and was due to leave shortly.

It was still raining making it difficult to get around the routes overland, we had to use the roads as cross country was impassable, even Kangaroos were finding it difficult not just because of the muddy conditions but at least one had been hit by the Schu-Mines. At 1a.m it was decided we would go by road, leaving Roggell back towards Uitwaterings Canal on to Helden to meet up in a large wooded area with the Gordon's. We experienced quite a lot of shelling around the River Maas area but no one was hurt. On the 24th November our troop carriers arrived to transport us to Levereuij just outside Nijmegen where we spent the night.

The next day we marched to a place we call the Island, known as the Island because it lies between the River Maas and the Rhine. It was very damp uninteresting place where we took over from the 101

US Airborne Division. The Island is only about 6 miles long by 4 miles wide inhabited by small farms.

The danger of this place is that it can be flooded if sluice gates from the river are opened by whoever is in control of them.

With this in mind it was pointless digging slit trenches as they could easily be filled with water so we had to build up some sangars. A sangar, as it is correctly known, is a temporary fortified position constructed of whatever materials are available, stones or sandbags creating protection when trenches are not possible or impractical. The enemy had planted Schu-Mines around the place. This became evident as we found the remains of the odd grazing cow that had made contact with them.

Looking around there was lots of livestock around so maybe we could look forward to special rations, but for now we settled for a supply of self-igniting canned foods we had used before during the landings and we welcomed some hot soup.

The island was accessible via a bridge not far from Nijmegan on the road to Arnhem; it had been captured and protected by the Americans who were under constant shell fire by the enemy.

In addition the Germans would send mines drifting down the river in a hope to hit the piers, this meant that the allied guards would not only dodge being hit by the shelling they would rifle fire at drifting mines in a hope to detonate them.

In the meantime, we were put on constant flood watch and briefed on rapid evacuation should the water levels rise to dangerous levels. Sometimes even in dangerous situations we get the giggles and often not knowing what you are laughing about, but one Jock piped up "I'm pissed off with water" and another replied "well, what do you want to piss"?

We were supposed to be watching out for German raiding parties but we are sat in a sanger rolling about with laughter.

The next day things changed somewhat, firstly the weather was cold and rainy in the Opheusden area of the island and we had the sad news that Capt. Herbertson and Sergeant Taylor had been badly injured by Schu-Mines. Not sure of the injuries but I presume they will have lost limbs as they both looked very seriously injured in the lower areas.

Basically everyone suffers when you get this type of news as we all think the war is almost over and you cannot help but think, one day we will be homeward bound to our families.

The truth is we will never let complacency take over and we will never be sure of our future until we are knocking on our parents' front door.

So we are feeling down and the water is rising around us, not much higher ground to take cover and you don't have to have brains to see where the livestock are going and that is where we were ordered to move. As we took cover for the night, one of the Jocks suggested we had a game of cards to take our minds off this dreadful environment.

Sat having a pot of tea and playing Rummy a conversation started on the subject of class distinction both at home and in the Army.

Civilian class for example in Yorkshire was basically, the rich, mill owners, farmers and land owners who were considered upper class, middle class were those who took management positions with mill owners also doctors, solicitors etc.

Then come the mass known as the working class who didn't know they were poor because everyone around them was the same. They had to settle for working in the mill or down the pit and accept jobs with little future. You only got to know how poor you were by comparing the lifestyle of the rich when given the opportunity to labour for them by gardening or washing their cars.

Most of the Jocks had the same opinion. Their parents were dockers, factory workers, again regarded as working class, in fact all of us privates were working class. The posh somehow were pre-selected for upper class posts, officers, captains; we didn't know any working class officers or upper class privates so we came to the conclusion that class distinction was evident in the army as well as civilian life. So now it came down to our position in the Army. Andy the Jock spoke out by saying "we privates are fodder, we are brainwashed to doing as you are told and never to question an officer"

The group agreed that officers live a cushy life, even during wartime, compared to privates.

Crombie piped in saying that he knew officers who sailed to Normandy, in first class having silver service when we were crammed into basic carriers for two days. Yes said Andy and they had nights out in Paris going to clubs and posh restaurants and do you know as we slept in tents outside Antwerp they went shopping for perfume and some stayed in hotels. That's nothing I said, me and Jim watched them playing golf, they must have brought clubs, and we knew the RE's hadn't totally cleared the golf course of mines but didn't bother telling them as it made watching golf more interesting. That brought a fit of laughter amongst the lads.

Jim added to the discussion by speaking up for his officer when he was a batman for a few weeks, he said his officer was more like a big brother. He protected him, gave him good rations and only got angry on minor things like the day he gave him a hard time because he had lost one of his handkerchiefs. Laughter again. "Well," said Andy, "I know lots of those officers drink a bottle of whiskey every day." Crombie added by saying, "Hey guys, they do get killed in action though." "Yes," said Andy "because they are either pissed or can't run as fast as us privates." After much deliberation we all agreed there was nothing we could do about it, decided to settle down for the night and attempt to keep warm as it was freezing and the damp coldness made it hard to settle down. We slept knowing of the dangers of rising water and the fact that German patrols were still in the area.

Next morning we got the news of the death of Major Wright and Major Monro, it was only a week ago we said goodbye to a great soldier, Major Wright who had served throughout the war and was ready to take a well-earned exit. However, they only got as far as Antwerp when they were hit by a V2 Rocket, how sad for two fine officers to go in such a tragic way, bearing in mind our conversation of last night. Still on the Island on 1st December, with flooding causing problems we had to consider a further move when we were informed that Major Smith-Cunningham had taken out a small party of men to recce a move about half a mile away. Not long after leaving Lieut. Scott and Captain Johnston returned, Scott was badly injured as they had been ambushed by a German patrol.

Unfortunately Smith-Cunningham had been captured by the Germans and taken prisoner, so with Lieut. Scott being out of action Captain Johnston took over the command of our Division.

Morale has taken a hit, the conditions were terrible the water was still rising at a rate of a few inches each day, you could see the roads were flooded and could only be identified by the telegraph posts. Things were obviously getting very serious and we needed to know where to move next and in a hurry.

A further recce was sent out to find an alternative sight. Things got more serious as it was clear that the Germans had opened the sluice gates and it was too late to march off the Island. Our only escape was to sail off the Island and by luck we had the assault boats available this time with small outboard motors. We all managed to escape to Heeswijk just outside Hertogenbosch, the place we were at a month ago.

On arrival we found the place crowded with troops, we were all absolutely shattered and welcomed the news that battalion was declared "Non-Operational" Giving us time to take a rest while replenishing our stores and updating our equipment.

We could not believe it, after all that rain and water it was now snowing.

Some of the lucky ones, including the Pipes and Drums, were invited to return to St Valerie-en-Caux to attend a special Fete of Liberation.

We stayed behind for further training and prepared for the next move. An important part of training included further recognition of the Schu-Mines, these were causing lots of injuries and our superiors recognised the importance of instilling into us how effective these small mines were.

After a few days of trouble free times you soon recover and start to feel positive again as there was no sign of the enemy, one could move around freely and mingle with the locals as you begin to relax and feel safe.

On the 15th December, once again, we had a visit from Field Marshal Montgomery he specifically came to Heeswijk to present awards to the members of the 51st who received decorations. Good to know a Private

Smith received an MM along with Cpl. Christison, Cpl. Greenhorn, and Sgt. Maxie, a DCM to Lieut. Fraser, a MC to Major Pilcher and a DSO and Bar to Major Dunn.

Monty then gave a speech telling us how well we were doing and that the Germans were on their knees and without petrol which would make it impossible for them to mount an offensive.

All this confidence building was taken lightly as there was contradiction in what we had been told during recent training.

General Rennie had told us that we were being prepared, in the New Year, to drive the enemy out of the Reichswald right back to the Rhine and into Germany.

At the same time we heard that Hitler had other plans as he intended to continue to battle south of our location in an effort to regain Brussels and Antwerp. If he succeeded this would cut the Allies in half and prevent us from moving forward towards the Rhine. Within a couple of days the Germans did in fact launch a drive under the command of General von Runsted with three Armies, the 5th and 6th Panzers and the 7th Army, they managed to break through the forward positions of the Americans but were halted at Hotton and Bastogne.

You are never sure how much of this gossip is true. Fighting was not on our minds as we were looking forward to Christmas and having some great social events with the locals who were in the same frame of mind. We were also awaiting details of the rota system planned for Christmas as leave could be granted depending upon the seniority of service since D-Day. I did not think Jim would be granted actual leave as he did have some leave while he was ill in July/August, if this is the case I am staying put as there is no way we are not celebrating Christmas together.

One of the good points of being in a HQ situation we get better services as today we collect our post from the UK and we managed to send Army issue Christmas cards home. Jim got a letter from his Dad saying the weather was bad in Yorkshire, it was cold dropping to -4 during the night, foggy and heavy snow in Scotland. His Dad mentioned Huddersfield Town had beat Leeds United 4-2 with two goals from Price, one from Glazzard and an own goal from Birch.

He had also found a couple of Jim's football cigarette cards in a drawer he included in the Christmas card. Just as we thought we were settled for a few days, we received orders to move to a Concentrated Area to prepare for the Reichswald operation on the 19th December. On arrival late that night we were told not to settle down long term as at first light we would be moving again to Louvain and on to Urmond.

The roads were heavily congested, moving slowly due to poor weather conditions, as we arrived in Urmond two days later. Our HQ was by coincidence, being Christmas, in an old monastery.

There was a joyful atmosphere as we were all prepared to celebrate Christmas during the next few days.

The Divisional Commanders message read out as follows.

I intended starting a week ago to visit every Company or equivalent in the Division and wish you a Happy Christmas and New Year and to thank you all for what you have done for the Highland Division, but events have made that impossible. I am afraid that Christmas will not be as well organised as it might have been, but I hope the food and drink turn up and you will all have as happy Christmas as can be under the circumstances.

The present German offensive has been, to a large extent, established and the flanks of break- through are firm so in the next few days we must expect a counter-offensive to be launched by the Allies, which should have far reaching results, results which we hope will shorten the War and make the task of forcing the defensive and river obstacles between us and Berlin easier. For the present we are serving under the command of General Simpson, who commands the 9th United States Army and we are held in reserve to counter-attack in the event of a German break-through on this front. General Simpson told me he was very proud to have the Division under his command and he knows of our great traditions. We must therefore be sure to deal with any tasks we are given in true HD fashion.

Another year of great achievements and deeds is drawing to a close and let us hope that next spring will see final victory and our tasks of bringing the Germans to utter defeat completed.

Good luck and a very Happy New Year to you all.

Very nice speech but it sounds like Christmas is not

going to happen as we are in reserve and it looks like the food has not turned up.

Christmas morning came so we accepted an invitation to join the locals at a church service in Urmond Protestant Church, we sang familiar hymns and received a warm welcome from the congregation. Unbeknown to us the grub had arrived and our cooks had worked relentlessly to prepare a fantastic meal, due at noon.

The Colonel-in-Chief of the Regiment, Her Majesty the Queen, had sent Christmas Puddings in a hope they would be served during Christmas dinner. Just a year ago we celebrated Christmas at home in Yorkshire and we had a great time with our loved ones and I got to meet Jim's family, that was special.

Yet in May we had no time to get back home during leave so it is just one year since we have seen our families. It seems years ago and we have crammed more into the last year than our lifetimes and we have seen so much of Europe.

We began to enjoy a wonderful meal there was even champagne being passed round, hell knows where that came from, and the atmosphere was unbelievable. The officers began to circulate round the tables to wish us all a Happy Christmas all in great form, the only thing missing was our loved ones and maybe a few party hats.

Just as we were thinking of having great booze up, at 2p.m an announcement came for us to be prepared for a move within the hour, they must be joking?

Food and drink started to vanish from the table as we

all consumed as much as we could take, let's hope we are not put in to action; surely even the Germans do not want to fight today.

Nobody was playing a joke as we were on route via Liege to Plaineveux by 3p.m. due to arrive early evening. When Boxing Day came we were noted as non-operational so it was decided to do a rerun of Christmas Day as many of the guys did not get chance to enjoy yesterday's celebrations. Food was served to the officers and cooks and to anyone who had missed out on the first session.

It was snowing and very cold, the snow getting deeper by the hour.

The locals started to celebrate and had painted welcome signs all over the building. They were flag waving and greeted us with much enthusiasm knowing that the dreaded Germans had fled. Maybe the Germans had fled but by midday, whilst we were having a Memorial Service for those comrades who had fallen since D-Day, the place was hit by V-2 rockets. The mood changed rapidly as the local population believed the enemy was returning they pleaded with us to protect them and to stay with them rather than moving on.

We assured them that we would not allow the Germans to return and the CO told them we had no intention of moving until the New Year.

Jim was a little quiet today as his thoughts were back home in Huddersfield, it was his mother's birthday. The weather is getting worse; snow is falling constantly so it seems unlikely we will be able to move on, even if this was the plan. The locals had been reassured and they became more relaxed and friendly, constantly offering to share any food and drinks they could spare and inviting us into their homes. No further raids from the Germans during the next few days giving the Jocks time to think about New Year's Eve.

In England we celebrate New Year but it is secondary to Christmas day but the Jocks, and there are loads of them, love their Hogmanay celebrations.

Bearing in mind we were awaiting further orders and could be moved at short notice the Jocks were told to keep the celebrations under control.

Yes we had a sing-song and glasses were raised but this was also a time to summarize the passing year with dreams of the coming year.

It has been a momentous year which we will always be linked with our arrival on the Normandy beaches and the dreadful battles through France, Belgium and Holland and now to the borders of Germany. Glasses were raised in memory of our brothers as we vowed that there would be no going back on their commitment and to ensure that their sacrifices were not in vain. God bless those fallen brothers.

Crossing a pontoon bridge on our way to Belgium from France

Welcoming from residents as we pass through Brussels

As we entered Holland we could see our paratroopers landing

September 1944 American planes towing gliders over Holland

The arrival in Eindhoven Holland September 1944

Moving into action October 1944

51st Highland Division Udenhout, 29th October 1944

Gordon Highlanders, during an assault in, October 1944.

Infantry take cover behind a building during an attack

Troops of 51st Highland Division, take cover

The drive on Hertogenbosch, October 1944

Keeping watch on the banks of the Maas River

Big problems, due to thick mud

After the rain came the snow, the camouflage wear
did not keep out the freezing cold

Our cooks work hard to prepare Christmas lunch

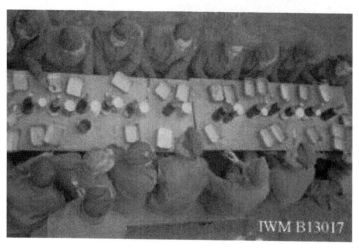

We await that very special Christmas Lunch,
notice the bottles of Champagne

Cigarette cards send from Jim's Dad of Jim's football heroes.

Army issue Christmas card 1944

What the papers say December 1944

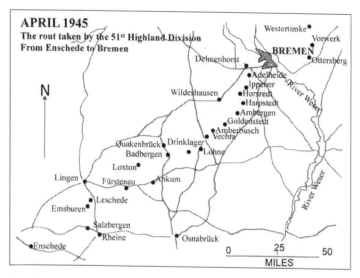

Our hopes for 1945, complete liberation of Holland, cross the Rhine
to Victory in Germany

HEADING FOR GERMANY

JANUARY 1945

As we entered the New Year 1945 at 2p.m. we were on the move, well attempting to move as the weather was dreadful. Our carriers were skidding all over the place, in fact ours skidded into a ditch and had to be hauled out, and fortunately no one was hurt.

We arrived in Dorinne, to our delight the billets were in the village were quite good and under cover. We were designated as an independent brigade in 30 Corps reserve.

Our Companies job was to stand by and to watch out as German parachutists had been spotted despite the falling of snow.

The superiors, who had gathered information by radio and reliable Recces, knew we were in for a tough time ahead and began to update us all on the forward plans that will include fighting in heavy snow conditions and possibly in wooded areas.

This we had been trained for in Scotland and many of the veterans in our Division had experience in 1941 and 1942 in Banchory and Forres.

There was a limited issue of all-white snow suits but to be honest, these were useless other than as camouflage. They didn't keep the cold out and were not suitable to wear a trench coat over the top.

We discussed tactics on how to prevent frostbite and more importantly how to stop your rifle bolts and mechanism from icing up.

It was so cold you have to struggle to keep your hands warm enough to operate the actions of the rifle and when you did manage to raise your weapon your eyes would be watering so much you could hardly identify the target.

Extra Weasel transports had arrived as they were more designed to cope with heavy-snow conditions. A Weasel is a British-designed tracked vehicle that can transport troops and is capable of towing anti-tank guns much more efficiently than standard carriers in the worst of snow conditions.

Much to the disappointment of our captain, many of the Weasels were unserviceable, however his team worked wonders in bringing them up to scratch and fit for purpose.

The place was overcrowded with Americans, not as popular with the Jocks as the Canadian guys. They were a bit cocky, believed they were better trained, and loud and overconfident. They did not have the awareness or consideration that some of our guys had been fighting for 5 years when they only landed seven months ago.

Many of our Canadian friends were of Scottish

descent and had in fact joined Canadian Scottish Regiments and we got on famously.

Talking to a group of Americans they told us of something they had experienced a couple of days ago, don't know if it's true, however, there was a group of Germans who had captured three Americans a few days earlier while doing a recce in a jeep, one of the Americans being an officer.

The Germans, now in ownership of a vehicle, uniforms and the correct paperwork, used their expertise in replicating American soldiers.

They even spoke in English but with American accents.

Their job was that of intelligence or sabotage communicating via radio back to their base. They managed to get behind our lines until they were stopped by an American guard on one of the bridges. They had everything needed by the guard but somehow his gut feeling made him suspicious so he asked for the password. Failing to know the word they could not give him an answer so he ordered them to get out of the jeep, which they did. He then approached the officer, gun pointing at him and told him to drop his trousers. Unwillingly at first, but still at the point of a gun, the officer dropped his trousers, by this time the guard had called for assistance.

With the man's pants down to his ankles, the guard told his private to check the label on the officer's underpants. The private was confused but he did as ordered, then realised why, the underpants had a German label.

The three were arrested and taken prisoner. We all had a good laugh when told the story but we also agreed that me and Jim, for instance, had never been abroad before, yet now we are surrounded by people from all over the place, Russians, Belgians, Dutch. We can't tell the difference between Dutch and German and now it proves that the paperwork is not always genuine, so who knows.

On 9th January we were on the move again to a place near Marche with a plan to move on up the valley alongside the River Ourthe towards Laroche.

The plan was to clear out the Germans who had attempted to enter Antwerp and the coast but failed. However they were causing massive problems by blocking roads, laying mines and felling trees to slow down any progress.

The area was very hilly with twisting narrow roads, many of them only tracks, made more difficult with the thick snow.

The Germans had time to establish themselves with tanks and Spandau posts giving them good vision, good field of fire, making us very vulnerable in the slow-moving snowy conditions.

Conditions got even worse as vehicles were getting stuck in snow drifts of 4ft or more. It was decided after a ration of hot soup that we would go by foot to the nearest village of Warvzy, in darkness, around 1a.m.

This gave time for our tanks to attempt to clear tracks

to enable other vehicles to get to the village. We had little opposition on the way to the village but somehow knew we were being watched by the enemy. On arrival we attempted to sleep but this was made difficult as there was a constant noise from the remaining members of the Division arriving by transport.

The next morning we began to receive a warm welcome from the villagers, it was the first time they had seen their Allies. They informed us that the Germans had only just left, in fact we could hear the German vehicles moving on the far side of the village. We were all freezing and hungry some of the lads were suffering physically from the extremely cold weather.

To our delight trucks arrived with hot food so we were able to tuck in and take a rest while planning the next move.

While retreating, the Germans had blown up the bridge on the road out of the village, they had blown craters in the roads, planted mines again making it too dangerous to move forward.

The Royal Engineers were sent ahead to try to clear the roads and rebuild the bridge, our job was to protect them through the night as they worked tirelessly.

By the 11th January they had rebuilt the bridge allowing us to move further toward Laroche then on to Roupage.

On arrival, having had a quiet journey, we found that the 1st Black Watch had held and secured Laroche. We could now move to the start line ready to climb the steep wooded area where we knew the Germans were in waiting.

The first Recce vehicle hit a land mine, then our Pioneer platoon began to clear the road of at least 30 trees which were blocking the path. They were followed by bulldozers, finally making it passable.

The first advance came from the Northamptonshire Yeomanry who moved forward with Sherman tanks, but which soon came under fire, knocking one Sherman out whilst another two struggled with mechanical problems. We were exposed as we could see the enemy at the top of a hill, they had taken over Farm du Vivier giving them a great advantage as we moved quickly to the right of a wooded area under Spandau fire. By luck we managed to hit and set alight a large haystack right in the centre of the attacking Germans, smoking them out of their advantage position. Meanwhile tracks had been partly cleared, allowing our anti-tank guns to take up attacking positions. After considerable resistance the enemy eventually retreated, however, we were aware that their shelling had caused many casualties.

Constant enemy fire kept any movement to a minimum. Again the weather was getting colder, we were pinned down, freezing, and food supplies could not be delivered.

With the temperature dropping to minus 32 degrees our equipment, including Bren guns, were frozen up. It was going to take every bit of strength we had to survive this situation. We had to force some of our lads from giving in as they were taken over by the cold and finding it difficult to even walk.

It's easy to imagine what it's like to be cold but this kind of cold hits all your joints, my knees are stiff it hurts to move yet if you don't stamp your feet and rub your hands and arms you feel as if your whole body is about to shut down.

Through that cold night there was one consolation, we could hear the German vehicles moving to a new position so maybe it would be safe to move the following morning.

We believe they had headed to Hubermont to consolidate ready for a further battle.

As soon as our position appeared to be stable we moved closer to the village to meet up and establish our HQ.

For what appeared to be ages we were able to take refuge in some barns and out buildings just outside the village, after battling it out with German Panthers.

It looked like the Gordon's had fought heavily, making our arrival not as difficult as their arrival and we could see we had lost many.

The sounds of battle had ceased as we gathered together to evaluate our situation. We were informed of the casualties to our Division during the last few days. 6 men killed, 30 badly wounded and over 40 suffering from frostbite and other cold related illnesses.

News came that we would head for Turnhout travelling via Laroche and we were promised good billets and a couple of days rest.

Much to our surprise we were billeted in the local school halls that gave us good warm cover and were able to take a well-earned rest.

Again we received a warm welcome from the residents, who turned out for a Battalion Church Parade in a monastery school, followed the next day by the Pipes and Drums 'Beat Retreat' entertaining an appreciative audience.

At the end of January we had experienced a peaceful situation for a few weeks and we set out to revisit Haaren. Last time in Haaren we had serious battles but this time, having liberated the place in October, should be more joyful.

I remember we had heavy casualties in October so hopefully when we return it may give us comfort that our efforts have been worthwhile.

There was a good atmosphere amongst the boys, it's amazing how quickly moods can change especially, when we are told victory is in sight.

On arrival in Haaren we were welcomed like heroes. The place had changed so much since October, it was still cold and a bit snowy but it did not stop the residents turning out to welcome us back.

It was announced that the residents had worked together in building a memorial in memory of the lads from 51st Highland Division who gave their lives during the liberation.

They were disappointed that it was not completely finished for our arrival but you could see that this was a priority.

Within a few days we were invited to a ceremony to unveil the plaque on the memorial, this was an emotional moment.

Backtracking our memories of the battles we had not far from Haaren, we recalled meeting the Yorkshire lass who married a Dutch farmer, we remembered some of the boys sadly lost and the time we shot the young German soldier. It was interesting to talk about how we had matured since October as we have seen so much and been in some frightening positions and somehow it becomes the norm, nothing much will shock us anymore.

The CO left for leave in the UK and command was taken over by Major Dunn who informed us that General Horrocks was due to visit on 29th January.

His visit was basically to update us on the present situation in Europe. Most of his visit was spent with Major Dunn, so we guessed he would be laying out plans for our future.

Our observations were correct, Major Dunn a few days later called everyone to an important briefing. He explained in detail that the postponed Exercise Veritable would commence early February as the weather was going to turn milder.

Major Dunn is a great motivator and confidence builder. He used large scale maps to explain the battle plan, due to commence in a few days.

He knew from intelligence that the enemy was building and preparing to stop the Allies entering Germany.

He wanted us all to be fully aware of our duties and that the next few days would be focussed on the Reichswald, then breaching the Siegfried Line giving an opening to the Rhine and for the first time entering German soil.

With this accomplished we would have a clear run to Berlin.

He concluded by saying that although things had been quiet recently, not to get complacent as the retreating Germans are waiting for us and that we have some tough fighting ahead of us.

The weather forecast was correct, the snow had gone, the skies had cleared and it was much milder, perfect time to move forwards.

On the 7th February we moved in Troop Carriers to Beers for an overnight stay before moving to an Assembly Area at Grafwegen.

The billets were OK but we had little chance to sleep as we were constantly bombing and shelling the German line to soften them up ready for our planned assault.

We were moved to the Start Line a placed called Pyramid Hill. The journey was difficult due to fallen trees and craters in the roads and therefore movement was slow.

The enemy was in waiting in the forest and we experienced lots of attacks but at the same time got the feeling the Germans were retreating south.

The main objective was to climb the hillside of the

wood forcing the Germans back and at the same time identifying where the source of fire was coming from. The enemy was hitting us with Spandau and Schmeisser as we struggled up the hillside through fallen branches and constantly diving for cover.

A small group advanced towards where they had spotted the source of fire and managed to see them off with grenades and Brens.

Reports came back that the enemy was on the run. By that time we had been joined by reinforcements, totally outnumbering the retreating opposition.

By late afternoon we had reached the hill top. We could see the enemy had just about ceased fire, we also managed to hit a horse drawn wagon carrying ammunition and towing a 150mm gun.

Orders came to establish our defensive positions and dig slit trenches and make sure we would not allow the enemy to cross our line.

Jim and I dug as deep as we could and surrounded ourselves with fallen branches as we were told not to allow the enemy to spot our positions. We were told smoking was not permitted as this is a giveaway. Our group was ordered to take turns on guard-duty while the others tried to get some sleep as there was still occasional fire from the enemy.

In total darkness in the forest, unable to talk to each other as we were told to stay silent, you felt vulnerable and too scared to sleep so we just waited until the morning. Any attempt to sleep was brought to a halt from the sound of snapping twigs or any sound you would normally expect in a night-time forest situation.

We were told not to open fire unless it was a hundred percent necessary, it was important not to allow the enemy to know our positions.

The Germans were not as clever, we could hear their voices and see the glow of cigarettes but this could also be a trick to lure us into exposing our positions so we refrained from firing and just held tight.

By day light our group had all survived the night with no casualties but lack of sleep and the fear of attack had stretched our nerves to the limit.

It has now been three days since we had a real night's sleep, we were all exhausted. The good news was that ahead of us, during the night, a patrol had gone out and shot up an important German signal HQ and the Germans had fled.

They had taken anti-tanks guns, lots of ammunition and captured almost 100 prisoners. We could see the quality of the opposition was not so great, they consisted of low grade, worn out, terrified young soldiers who appeared to be relieved by their capture. Our job had been successful in the forest, we did have casualties when climbing the hill but the damage we had done to the enemy was praised by our superiors. During the previous evening some of our boys had managed to have a hot supper of a delicious meat stew. We had missed out as we were ahead in slit trenches, much to our amazement there was still plenty leftovers so we, being starving, had a healthy helping for breakfast.

Around 10a.m on 9th February we were ordered to move out of the forest to capture Kanonskamp along a road with flood waters either side.

We had news that our colleagues, attacking the Siegfried Line from the northern side by the banks of the Rhine, had experienced problems with the change in weather and thawing had caused deep mud conditions bogging them down as tanks and other vehicles could not advance to support the attacks.

Our own RAF had destroyed much of the roads making it impossible for the 15th Scottish Division to capture the town.

On route to Kanonskamp we were hit by heavy fire from the North-West side , smoke screens were put up to maintain our cover, however, we suffered 15 casualties with 2 killed.

We then entered and secured the town by mid-afternoon as we met up with the Gordon's who had approached from the right hand side of the town.

We were looking forward to a real sleep, tired and drained from the cold night in the forest, when we were told Colonel Bradford was returning from leave tomorrow.

Knowing he would be fresh and keen to give orders for the next move we were determined to have a good rest.

True to form early the next morning the plan was to attack Gennep.

Gennep was a textile industrial town on the Dutch

border, once heavily occupied by Jewish workers who had either fled or been taken to concentration camps. Our approach to the town would be via a night crossing of the Niers and to attack the town at dawn as the Germans had blown up the road bridge across the river.

D Company went ahead to cross the river and establish a bridgehead and a start line for us to follow.

We crossed the river on motor driven assault boats and headed for an Assembly Area when we came under fire from a German Patrol. They quickly abandoned their attack when we successfully shot and killed at least two them.

Day after day we are experiencing the same response from the Germans, they put up a fight while often retreating then realise they are outnumbered and beaten, they don't want to die so they give themselves up.

We are taking prisoners like never before, sometimes more than 100 in a day.

We were told that the civilians of Gennep had been evacuated due to the heavy bombings and it would be likely that anyone left in the town were probably Huns.

We approached Gennep from the northern side via trenches that had been dug by the Germans, the Gordon's from the south side by the railway station.

Our first sight was of a town in ruins, with lots of hideout positions for the enemy so our objective was to clear all the buildings, starting down the main street. We were immediately hit by about 50 Germans on entering the town. Johnstone, who was leading us, made a brave advance with his Sten gun scanning and firing at the enemy who scattered in all directions.

We would move slowly in small numbers covering the gaps between buildings by using smoke grenades, then entering each property in search of the Huns. In addition our NCO needed to be confident that we were driving the enemy away from the river bridge, allowing Sappers to repair it without being hit by snipers, thus allowing transport to cross the river.

Most of the buildings were badly-damaged, windows had been blown out which gave us good entry and vision.

We could see that a small group of Germans had entered a shop building about 50 yards away at a road junction, others had run down the main street. Sergeant Johnstone led us into the building, we were attacked by the Germans but he gave them little chance by killing two with such brave leadership.

The rest of them ran off by the back door, hedge hopping over the back gardens into another building, joining others as they began to counter attack using bazookas and grenades. Looking around I could see our group were clear of casualties and we were able to take cover firing at the building.

We started to lob grenades into the windowless openings, by this time the Germans decided they had had enough and gave themselves up.

Those who fled were running into the Gordon's who were well set up by the railway station. The enemy did manage to hit the Gordon's HQ, killing one soldier and injuring many.

We took orders to settle for the night, hold our positions and await the arrival of DUKW's that were crossing the river and ferrying essential transport to strengthen our resources.

We received reports that the Gordon's were in fact having difficulties in holding and protecting the railway station, this would be our first priority early the next day.

Not a bad few day's work as we managed to capture 174 prisoners.

Intelligence informed us that the enemy was holding out in an estate on the south side of Gennep and we should prepare for further battles ahead.

Early on the 12th of February our objectives were to fully capture the area in and around the railway station allowing the Gordon's to travel south protecting the railway lines down to Heyen.

Tanks and Crocodiles had arrived, thanks to the work done by the sappers on the river bridge, giving us a strong force when attacking the station area.

On approach to the station we received heavy shelling as the Huns were well prepared having secured a couple of buildings.

The first building we took with ease, killing a few Germans, but the second enemy post was about 200 yards away and we were exposed on approach. Again with good leadership we charged the building dodging bullets and everything they tried to give us. We were soon under cover outside the building. The first contact in the building we came face to face with a German Captain who was not prepared to surrender so we shot him dead.

To our surprise there were only about 10 Germans left and they, knowing we had their captain, gave in with little resistance.

Sadly we discovered we had casualties with maybe twelve deaths from the 5th Div. including Major Beales and Lt. McDonald.

The railway station and level crossing was secured so we had achieved our objectives allowing the Gordon's to journey to Heyen.

We were well praised on our efforts by our superiors as it would appear Gennep was a very important town to take over, being the road centre that would open up the western route into Rhineland.

That evening we managed to take it easy and relax. We got news that Huddersfield Town had played Oldham Athletic home and away, on 3rd February they won 3-2 with all 3 goals from Billy Price.

Then on 10th Town won 6-1 with goals from Baired, Glazzard, Watson and would you believe it 3 goals from Billy Price.

Jim was over the moon with the results, only to be reminded by the Jocks that Town and Billy Price were only doing well because the good players were at war leaving amateurs to play local games.

Even so it was good to know how well Town had performed all season and the fact that despite the war Town had attracted a crowd of 7,000 for the home game against Oldham.

We talked about what a tough couple of weeks we have had starting at Reichswald in that cold forest, charging up that bloody hill under fire, then onto Gennep and the fact that the Germans are fighting but not managing to win anything.

We moved on to a serious conversation started by Sam Durie who is a gambling man and always mentions "the odds" in conversation. If we were talking about the weather for example he would say bet you 5 to 1 the rain stops for more than 6 hours tomorrow.

We talked about our chances of seeing the war out and going home.

It is not just a case of staying alive, many guys will go home but with lifelong injuries including lost limbs, and some with mental problems overlooked by medics.

In the 5th Battalion alone we left for Normandy last June with a force of 900 men, we have had replacements due to injuries and deaths but it would be interesting to know how many of the 900 have survived.

For sure the 5th have lost 250 men in 7 months and the amount of injuries must be at least double.

The expert Sam came up with the odds, he started by stating that we were told the war would be over by Christmas and it's February. We have only just reached the borders of Germany so forecasting is almost a waste of time.

He figured out that the chances of being killed are about one in five and two in five of being injured. "If you are lucky," said Durrie "about half of us will go home in one piece."

Jim told us about his cousin who was picked up in Dunkirk in 1940 who was physically fit when he returned home but was not mentally fit and to this day he lives with the results of the war.

Randomly he sleepwalks, gets out of bed and wanders off in the night. He has been found hiding in people's gardens early in the morning not having a clue how he got there.

His brain must tell him he is unsafe and needs to take cover, how long this will continue nobody knows and it is not well-publicised as if the army want to keep it low key.

Unfortunately death becomes the norm, grief and sorrow may come later but right now emotions are numbed by daily deaths.

We decided that was enough for one day.

We spent most of the morning clearing up around the station and odd houses overlooking the railway embankment and continued to help clear the road to Hummerum.

Rain continued making the exit from Gennep more difficult due to flooding.

The enemy were still holding out in various buildings along the road, as we were fired upon sustaining casualties including the death of Lt. Foster.

On the 18th we received orders to a Concentration Area in Asperden in preparation for a night attack on Goch.

Goch, like Gennep, was a key target being a major link in the Siegfried Defensive Line and still held by a strong German defence.

The Germans had assumed any attack would come from the main road into Goch from the South side so they were well prepared.

Not sure whether it was luck or perfect tactics as we approached from the North, a more difficult route along the side of the River Niers.

We entered the outskirts of the town in the darkness around 1a.m before the enemy realised so there was little resistance as we approach the first buildings. There appeared to be some activity in a factory on one side of the street but most of the buildings had suffered from heavy bombardment. We were ordered to look for Germans in the cellars.

Our usual technique was to lob a grenade down the cellar steps and take cover before entering to inspect the damage. Someone came up with a novel way to seek out the enemy which was less messy, we would toss a brick down the cellar steps and wait with our rifles in readiness. It worked wonders, within seconds any living Hun would come charging up the steps when we would give them the option of surrender or death.

Within an hour we had a bag full of prisoners, however we were taken by surprise as some Germans had dug in around the back gardens, a few wanted to fight but many gave in when outnumbered.

One of our lads came running round the corner shouting "Gas, Gas, they are hitting us with gas". A few went to investigate but found that shelling had hit a Jerrycan full of petrol filling the place with smoke. Once clear it revealed that two of our drivers had been killed in the explosion.

Our reinforcement was delayed as a damaged bridge could not take the weight of anti-tank guns and even jeeps had problems in getting into town.

At this stage of the attack we were confident we could manage as the main qquare was in sight and we were coping with any enemy response.

Beyond that was a church and what looked like a hospital building. The enemy, taking refuge in the church, were driven out as they took cover in the hospital.

In the courtyard some prepared for fighting, firing at us, but we knew it was only delaying their capture.

No bricks this time, our lads went in with grenades followed by Sten gun attacks. Very soon we could hear the cries of Germans coming from the basement of the church and we were ordered to cease fire.

The first one to appear was a German officer next to one holding a white flag, followed by around 20 soldiers.

The officer was badly injured and was shown great respect by our NCO as he supplied a stretcher and helped him on to it. Then ordered his men to carry him away for treatment escorted by some of our Jocks. Now most lads in charge of this situation would have shot the Germans as they came out of the basements but our NCO knew we were well-covered as we had planted our snipers covering the crossroads by the church so we were relatively protected from attack.

As we had our snipers all over the place you could assume that there would be other Germans hiding and watching the situation.

Those Germans in hiding and watching the compassion of our leader realised they would not be shot on surrender, unlike the actions of their SS men. Very soon they began to trickle out with hands above their heads making a total of over 400 prisoners in the past 10 days.

By early evening our supplies and transport had arrived and we awaited the arrival of the Gordon's, ready to pass through and move southward towards Thomashof, south-west of the town.

The battle of Goch was not over, although we had done well in clearing the initial area, there were still plenty of Germans in town and many moving south of the town and preparing for our next advance. We kept movement to a minimum during the night as there was an increase in activity from the enemy, we were being shelled as we took cover in the ruins and there was still the odd sniper knocking about.

In addition they were hitting us with "Moaning Minnie's" a name for the German Nebelwerfer mortar.

Whilst taking cover there is always time for a laugh as we compared experiences of the day when a Jock, told us one of his lads had entered a building backwards while under sniper fire. Closing the door and in darkness he backed onto what he thought was a white ghost, it was in fact a tethered white horse. He was so terrified he wet his pants but the horse was in a worse state as it had gone mad with the sounds of battle. In fear of being cornered he decided he would rather face the snipers than a mad horse.

The Jocks always have a story to tell, truth or not this story went down well.

By now the Gordons had arrived and would take a rest before going ahead of us through the south part of town

After a couple of days we realised we had under estimated the Germans, they had in fact continued to hammer us and we got the feeling we were against a better case of soldiers determined to defend Hitler's Reich.

They now resisted every attack and counter attack, fighting tirelessly something we have not seen for months.

Goch is going to take a lot longer to overcome than we believed earlier.

German patrols were masters of the art with continuous shelling and sniper skills making it very difficult to move. We were pinned down just dreaming of blankets to keep us warm and a hot meal as Goch became a living hell.

Battling furiously for ten days with sleepless nights

due to deafening explosions, the skies engulfed with flames, the cries and screams of our injured colleagues made life impossible.

We are so thankful to XXX Corps and the Welsh Division in helping us get the upper hand when we were able to withdraw and move to a village to take refuge for a few days recuperation.

The boys were so relieved to be out of the action, billeted in some wrecked buildings for a rest and declared "on reserve".

We were congratulated on our performance as it was announced that Captain Johnstone had been promoted to major and took command of D Company.

Tom Renouf a friend of ours who we met at training in Perth was promoted to corporal, this came as great news as he is only our age. He joined the Tyneside Scottish and was transferred to the 5th a few months ago.

Like Jim he was returned home with injuries yet recovered to re-join us in Holland. He is a good soldier and wherever there is a piano he is keen to entertain us with his wide variety of music.

On the 25th February a Warning Order came detailing an attack south-west of Thomashof clearing the area down to the river.

We are to be moved to an Assembly Area then cross the Start Line just before midnight, our biggest obstacle was flooding most of the area being waterlogged.

Immediately under Spandau fire from a post this was quickly taken out bravely by a Canadian leading the attack, who sadly lost his life.

We were directed towards the village of Robbenhof taking cover in farm buildings. We had trouble from a German pillbox but this was taken out, allowing us to move to attack the enemy who were well dug in on the river bank.

We took several prisoners who were in hiding in small outbuilding, killed a few fighters but sadly also lost a few of our guys.

Soon we had cleared the river bank making it possible for the RE's to make a start of clearing the main road of mines.

The first carrier was blown up slowing the operation down, they managed to drag the carrier into a ditch before moving off down the road.

Today has been a success, despite our losses. Have killed many and taken at least 100 prisoners. We will hold this position before being moved South of Goch to a Rest Area.

Things quietened down as March arrived. The division was in good condition, we were told to clean up and prepare for a visit by the Prime Minister.

On 4th March the Rt. Hon Winston Churchill arrived along with Field Marshal Montgomery and other officials.

The Pipes and Drums Beat Retreat Division came together with the Pipe Majors of all Divisions, creating a wonderful atmosphere.

Churchill addressed our Division and gave mention that we had fully avenged the old 51st downfall of 1940 and that he wanted us to know that we were second to none in the British Army.

Everyone appreciated his words and we all felt we should be proud of this significant occasion it being the first time our Pipes and Drums have performed on German soil.

HQ was set up in a in a new location, Groenenberg and the surrounding villages of Thorn and Wessen on the border with Holland.

We laughed when one of our German-speaking lads translated a leaflet that had been distributed by the Brits as propaganda directed at German women. The leaflet looked as if it had come from the German Government.

It basically told all women that it was their responsibility to make babies as Germany would need to increase the birth rate for the future.

It informed married women that despite their husbands being away they should feel it their duty to have children and this would not give grounds for divorce after the war.

This appeared to work as the females were more than friendly when inviting us into their homes. Imagine what this would do for the morale of those German soldiers away from home.

Our billets varied as many of us stayed in local houses, Jim and I were lucky as we found a family environment in a humble home much like ours in Yorkshire.

A kind lady with two children gave us open house,

the kids gave up their bedrooms for us without complaint, and at last we had warm beds.

We rewarded the family with supplies of bully beef and chocolate much more valuable than currency. A few days of total relaxation, drinking, socialising, bit of football and other games really made us think more about home.

Over a nice bottle of homemade Elderberry wine, supplied by our landlady, Jim and I talked about what we will do when the war is over and it's time for returning home. Jim opened by saying he would like to arrive home on Thursday afternoon take a bath and change into civvies then spend time with his family.

Yes I said and catch up on reading the Huddersfield Examiner and Brighouse Echo top to bottom.

OK then on Friday we will call in at the George in Brighouse and the Grey Horse, have a few beers, down to the Chippie for haddock and chips. Then on Saturday go and watch Town play Barnsley or whoever and thrash them 6 nil, yes, and Glazzard and Price both get a hat trick.

After the game we will go and get rat-arsed in Huddersfield and have a fish and chip supper.

"OK," I said "but you've forgot the girlfriends". "But they don't like football" said Jim.

Whatever, we have bonded forever and so look forward to a normal life back home in the not so distant future.

In Army life you get to know the term "Calm before the storm"

Rules have been relaxed for a reason, we are all aware that the next 10 days or so is about training and planning to cross the River Rhine, a key obstacle preventing real penetration into German territory.

Our superiors are busy running around to meetings, studying maps and on the 9th they had a big conference followed by a briefing to our officers.

On the 11th came our briefing when we were told that intensive training would commence immediately and would include night time practising crossing the River Rees in preparation to cross the Rhine.

Our first attempt was a shambles, just as we set off for the river a thick foggy mist came down and visibility was so poor we lost each other and Buffaloes lost their bearings. We did however manage to complete the training and the practise crossing without further problems during the days that followed.

So Operation Plunder is about to commence and it had been announced that the Highland Division have been chosen to lead the crossing.

Calls by some of "s........bring on the cannon fodder, we'll be the first ones hit by machine-gun fire"

On the whole, deep down, we felt very proud that we have been given this honour to be first across the Rhine.

We were told that recces had been made, our crossing places had been decided and that massive Artillery support, smoke screens would cover the area. We had backup from air support, who would implement heavy bombing raids prior to our crossing. All in all we were brimming with confidence and ready for action. The day before we left the local landladies and villagers had clubbed together and invited us to party with them sharing their meagre rations.

Out came the homemade local wine, cherry tarts, apple slices and although it was difficult to communicate we made it clear how happy it made us and at the same time many of them were tearful knowing of our departure.

On the 21st March we moved to a village, Marienbaum about 2 miles on the South side of the Rhine. During the evening, recces were sent out to confirm all was well on the river banks ready for crossing. They were spotted and the enemy brought down accurate mortar fire just to let us know they were in waiting.

During the next day our smoke screening covered the whole of the area and the artillery kept a steady fire on selected targets keeping the enemy away from crossing areas. Reporting back they had not found Schu-Mines or booby-traps so the approach would be relatively safe.

A strict timetable was adhered to in loading Buffaloes and we were in great form and eager to take part in such a historic crossing due at 2100 hrs.

On the 23rd we moved off as we headed only 800 yards from the banks of the Rhine, our artillery were bashing away like mad, the noise was horrendous. It was a beautiful sunny spring like day, blue skies a great contrast to what hit us in January and February.

At exactly 2100 hrs our Buffaloes began the advance to the river, there was an amazing atmosphere soldiers singing, pipes playing, we were so confident and excitement was at fever pitch.

Our crossing was about 450 yards quite wide for a river, we entered the water and quickly arrived safely on the far bank. Amazing how they unloaded us and rushed back to pick up more soldiers.

We knew our job was to form a bridgehead and secure the roads, surprising no mines on the river banks but they were found on the roadside.

Looking back we could see the activity on the river building up with Buffaloes, DUKW's and Storm Boats shuttling troops across the river.

There was some shelling but we seem to be holding off any counter attacks. Their attacks were not too intense, allowing our boys to cross easily.

This allowed the Royal Engineers to get busy building a bridge to span across the river that would bring supplies on various vehicles.

Once the road had been declared mine free we started to move in towards Esserden. When they said mine free, some were too deep to detect and resulted in a couple of Carriers being blown up.

The Gordons were to attack the town of Rees from the south, we were waiting to hear how they were going before moving off to the North side of Rees. They had been delayed slightly as the banks on the Southside were very worn and difficult to negotiate.

The next day we advanced to Rees where we attacked a strongly held factory building but managed to secure it relatively easily and pick up prisoners.

In addition almost every building we checked contained Germans ready to surrender without a fight. When we reached a cross roads we were hit by the enemy but again we managed to see them off, it's looking like they are giving in.

As we were preparing for our next move we got the terrible news that General Thomas Rennie (the boss) had been killed.

He had crossed the Rhine to check out how the battle was going at the sharp end and on his return was hit by a Mortar bomb.

Everyone was shocked and for Jim and me more so as we had spoken to the great man during training about a year ago.

HQ was set up in a municipal building as we gathered as confirmation came of all anti-tank guns and essential supplies were in place.

It's strange as we are picking up prisoners there is a mixed bag, some come out of hiding with hands in the air, others want to fight to the death and today we found some in a cellar on their knees praying we would not shoot them.

They must think the war is over and we certainly do.

Eventually we reached Isselburg on the 28th when billets were found in local farms still being heavily shelled but nothing too serious.

It was time to count our losses which were greater than we originally believed.

We had 56 casualties in total including 11 deaths in the last 7 days.

Brigadier Oliver took command until the arrival of General MacMillan who would replace General Rennie.

On the 31st we received a message from Sir Miles Dempsey, Commander of the 2nd Army. It read:

Now that the battle of the Rhine has been won and the break-out from the bridgehead is well under way, I would like to give you and your wonderful Division my very sincere congratulations. Yours was one of the two Divisions which carried out the assault crossing of the river, defeated the enemy on the other side, and paved the way for all that followed.

A great achievement and I am sure you are all very proud of it.

Our Canadian Allies in snow suits January 1945

6th Airborne Division Sniper wearing snow camouflage January 1945

Our Canadian Allies in snow suits January 1945

A 5.5 inch gun in action in the snow January 1945

Approaching Reichswald Forest February 1945

Churchill tanks arriving at Reichswald Forest

Dug in for the night Reichswald Forest

Sherman tanks arriving at Goch February 1945

5th Black Watch Sniper in action Gennep February

Preparing for the assault on Goch February 1945

The Welsh pass through the 51st Highlanders Goch February

A Churchill and Valentine Tank in Goch February 1945

Artillery fire across the Rhine in preparation
for our crossing March 1945

51st Highlanders are the first to cross the Rhine March 1945

Buffaloes during the Rhine crossing 24th March 1945

Douglas Dakotas heading for the drop zone of the
River Rhine March 1945

Winning the battle on the enemy side of the Rhine March

Taking German prisoners after the crossing 24 March

The Lambeth Bridge built within days of the crossing March 1945

Winston Churchill inspects the progress of the
Rhine crossing March 1945

The Daily Mail, 23rd March 1945

The Daily Mail, 24th March 1945

Courtesy Black Watch Museum

MAJOR GENERAL T. G. RENNIE had been killed in action in Germany and the 51st Highland Division has lost an outstanding-commander and the British Army has lost a great soldier. General Rennie's military career was an outstanding record of positive achievement. He escaped from the Germans after being captured with the original 51st Division at St. Valery, he commanded a battalion of his own regiment (The Black Watch) with great distinction in the battle of Alamein, he commanded an assault Brigade (154 Infantry Brigade) in the landings in Sicily, he commanded one of the two British assault Divisions in the landings in Normandy and, having been wounded a few days after D Day, he took over the 51st Highland Division before the break-out from the Caen bridgehead before commanding that Division right through France, Belgium and Holland, into Germany and across the Rhine. He was killed shortly after he himself had crossed the Rhine and had satisfied himself that the assault crossing by his Division had been successfully accomplished and that the operation was being developed in accordance with his plans.

THE FINAL DAYS TO VICTORY

April started with a rest period in Isselburg. There was a good feeling amongst the lads, we were a bit confused as there was a lot of appointments at officer level being made, but at this stage it would not affect us so we were not concerned.

Under the command of the Canadian Army we were briefed on our activities for the next month or so. The plan is quite basic, we are to travel north about 300 miles north to Bremerhaven with clear objectives.

Firstly RE's will be clearing roads and rebuilding bridges, it is our job to give them protection.

We should be constantly aware of mines planted by retreating Germans.

Now in Germany we need to be aware that all civilian-looking people are not necessarily to be trusted as we have trusted the Dutch: they may be the enemy.

We are unlikely to encounter strong resistance, however, we must not get complacent as there are still sporadic attacks from determined, retreating Germans along the route.

We moved on the 6th to Schuttorf with no problems on route and arrived at 1a.m to learn the town had already been captured hours before.

The roads in and out of Schuttorf were made

difficult due to fallen trees and mines delaying the progress of rebuilding a bridge on the Emsburen road.

During road-clearing we were attacked by small-arms fire from a wooded area it was obviously coming from only three points so we guest it was a few stragglers but they were doing a job of delaying our progress.

Whilst taking cover, two of our lads detonated Schu-Mines. They were injured but both still alive as they were stretchered back to base.

Eventually we managed to clear the area and the river bridge was repaired but we were told not to advance as the enemy were putting strong resistance on the Emsburen side of the river.

Our job was to clear the way as the Gordons were to pass through during the night. Indeed they did, in force, clearing the enemy and capturing Emsburen by dawn.

All is quiet in Schuttorf so we have a day off tomorrow before moving on.

8th April, what a great day, the sun was shining there is a feeling that spring has finally arrived.

We started the day with a good wash-down and shave followed by a brew of fine tea and hot toast made on an open fire.

We were told that today was going to be a day of relaxation, time to write home, catch up on kit cleaning and preparing for our next move to Ankum. By 10a.m. there was talk of a football match, not against anybody in particular but just anyone who wanted a kick around.

There was a flat, green grass playing field by the

school, almost in the centre of Schuttorf, right opposite a cafe where we could have a sample of German beer after the game.

German beer is an acquired taste; we would call it lager, bit like a shandy without the lemonade taste. It didn't have a frothy head like Webster's or Tetley's but when chilled it satisfied your thirst.

The Jocks laid out a challenge, bearing in mind we were outnumbered, and they insisted that we played at noon and it would be Scotland versus England on the school playing fields, now christened Hampden Park, and the losers would pay for the beers.

We only just managed to drum up a team of English as the Jocks would not allow us to recruit the Welsh or any other countries available.

The Jocks had a strong side as at least two of them played for the Incognitos Battalion team.

Not wishing to be belittled by the Jocks we accepted the challenge and began to discuss our team tactics.

Smithy, a quiet sort of guy over 6-feet-tall, announced that he in fact played as a professional for Aston Villa before the war broke out and this gave us some confidence. Private Miller then said he had played non-League with Harrogate, now he was built like a bulldog and just as aggressive, he looked like a boxer who had been hit with a cricket bat.

Keen to get to the game we all marched, taking care to spot any suspicious-looking mine areas.

As it was a warm day, and we had no football kits, the Jocks would play topless and we would play in white vests.

There were no line markings and we took some wooden stakes to act as goal posts and corner flags and agreed that anything above straight arms would be over the bar.

We could not agree on a referee as the only ones to offer were either Jocks or English.

11:30a.m. came and as we walked the half mile or so to the ground together the Jocks already telling us to prepare for a thrashing.

On arrival we decided to play 30 minutes each way.

We were just about to kick off when the school caretaker joined us and insisted he was a qualified football official so now we had a German referee. By this time we had a crowd gathering of locals and some of the lads from our camp.

The Jocks kicked off; as their front men dashed forward a little guy chipped the ball over our defence right in the path of their bustling centre forward who, without even controlling the ball, blasted it at goal giving no chance for our keeper. In fact our Aston Villa keeper was still pacing the goal line out unaware the game had started.

So the Jocks are one up and looking so confident on the ball, moving it around with precision first-time passes.

We managed to defend well, holding them back until half time, when the locals had brought cold refreshments. The crowd was building by the minute.

The second half started much the same until our

Miller did an over-the-ball tackle on their star man, putting him to ground. Fists started to fly as the Jocks reacted to the foul but the referee calmed things down using broken English.

Unfortunately the Jock could not continue and he was carried off the pitch, while luckily the referee only gave a free kick and allowed Miller to stay on the pitch.

Our keeper took a ball, bouncing it to the end of his assumed area, and kicked it the full length of the field where it bounced once as their keeper came out to take it but Jim, standing in front of the keeper, managed to back head it in to the goal making it one all.

Now this rattled the Jocks, who were now down to ten men and angered that we had equalised so soon after the restart. They began to play really rough tactics, kicking our guys at every opportunity.

With about five minutes to go our Johnson was pulled down while in a scoring situation and the referee gave a penalty. Miller was the first one up shouting, "I'll take it".

Nobody objected as Miller agreed with the ref where the penalty spot should be. He placed the ball took three paces back and blasted the ball giving their keeper no chance.

He hit the ball so hard it travelled about fifty yards into a stream and floated rapidly downstream into a wooded area. We only had one ball and it could not be retrieved, however this was put right when one of the locals tossed in a new ball after about five minutes. So now we are 2-1 up as the new ball was placed on the centre spot, the Jocks kicked off, the referee immediately blew the final whistle, the game was over.

The Jocks surrounded the referee claiming injury time for the time Miller fouled putting them down to ten men and the fact it must have taken five minutes to get a new ball after the penalty.

There was a bit of a language problem but the ref picked up the ball and marched off the pitch confirming that the game was over.

We wanted to get off the pitch as soon as possible, sensing there was a fight brewing and, although we agreed with the Jocks, it was to our advantage to accept the referee's decision.

Off we went to the cafe as planned to take in a few beers and celebrate our winning.

Now this is when you see the true character of the Jocks, they played like animals in the second half yet by the time we got to the cafe they were shaking hands and accepting defeat with such dignity. They were first to the bar ordering ale for everyone, never complained about the events during the game and just accepted the result. This I think was a wonderful showing of sportsmanship.

The beer started to flow as the owner refused to take any money and began to hand out plates of sausages and cold meats, the place filling with the local residents who joined in the party atmosphere. We heard news from one of the guys that Huddersfield beat Hartlepool 7-1 the day before, with two goals from Glazzard and, yes, five from Billy Price.

We gave a congratulation toast to Jim for scoring a goal, Huddersfield winning and the fact that today is two years to the day that Jim signed up for the army in Huddersfield.

What was surprising that the locals were really friendly as Schuttorf being so close to the border of Holland had received heavy bombing when the Allies would unload bombs on their way back to Britain. In addition the Allies had bombed and demolished their town hall only yesterday.

Many civilians had lost their lives during the bombings yet they were very friendly and made it clear that they hated Hitler and the horrible things he had known to endorse.

Surprisingly, the farms were worked by many different nationalities including Polish, French, Dutch and even Russians amongst those were German deserters who would be arrested if found.

It was around 5 p.m. when we staggered back to HQ to the Jocks leading the singing of songs only some of which we knew.

Back at camp we had a relaxing trouble free evening.

The next morning 9th April, Jim, myself and five other guys were ordered to assist the RE's and Pioneers in clearing fallen trees and Schu-Mines in other areas around the town, a job we had done a few days ago on the main roads.

It was obvious that random mines had been planted as there was evidence of livestock being struck by Schu-

Mines. The odd dead but fresh pig would not go to waste. We entered a field that had a large pond with a cart track running up the side leading to a main road. This was a shortcut into town as we could see fresh tyre tracks but it looked an obvious place to plant mines. The Pioneers were digging them up by the dozen and carefully placing them at the side of the track.

We knew little about these mines other than the fact that the detonator would be activated from the top of the box where there was a plunger, so careful handling was needed.

The corporal in charge was the only one with in depth knowledge of this type of mine, as he demonstrated how they should be handled.

We were uneasy as there was so many planted every few yards up the cart track, when we got to the top of the field we turned to see we had uprooted about 20 mines.

The corporal made the decision to carefully take the mines to the edge of the pond and with two men holding the Schu we were to swing our arms and let go at the count of three tossing the mine in to the water.

The first one exploded on contact with the water and no one was hurt, we just got drenched.

I told the Corporal I was unhappy with this procedure as it was not textbook and that we should leave it to the experts and maybe seek advice on the disposal. He replied, "They are much safer in the pond than on the track side so continue to do as you are told." We carefully collected all the mines from the track and placed them side by side ready to launch them into the pond.

I could see one of the local farmers waving at the top of the field holding a large bucket, I guess he was offering us a drink of something, which would be prefect as it was warm and we were in shirt sleeves and gasping for a drink. We agreed that I should go and find out what the man was offering so I wandered to the top of the field to collect the bucket.

The farmer could not speak English but showed me the content of his bucket which was filled to the top with beer whilst his hands were full of metal cups. Gosh what a prize, I could not wait to get back to the lads.

The thing was heavy as I carried it back and the beer overflowed down my trouser leg but there was still enough left to please everyone.

I had travelled about 25 yards when there was an almighty explosion down by the pond as one of the Schu's had detonated resulting in a mass of explosions as the whole lot went up.

Bodies were being thrown all over the place.

I dropped the beer and charged towards the pond as I could clearly hear the screams from my injured colleagues.

On arrival I could see all six men were grounded, with blood all over the place, and with little movement except for two of them.

The first man I reached was Jimmy Bruce who was clearly dead, along with Finlay and Strachan. The two other guys were injured badly but still alive. Then, face down, was Jim. I carefully turned him over to offer whatever care I was capable of giving him. I was on my knees with Jim nestled in my arms; his eyes were open as I told him everything would be OK. The explosion had alerted others, I could see stretcher bearers running up the field.

They quickly attended to the injured and confirmed that the three were in fact dead.

I screamed at them to attend to Jim, who was only concussed, whilst still nestling him in my arms. Jim looked at me as he slowly shook his head as if he knew his time was up.

His eyes slowly closed as he took his last breath, his face was perfect and unharmed by the explosion as he had taken the heavy blasts to his stomach area.

The medic put his hand on my shoulder and softy whispered "Sorry he has gone."

I lay on the ground rolling from side to side pleading for him to be alive but it was too late.

I had lost my very best friend. We had planned so much for our future in Huddersfield but now it was not to be.

I was filled with guilt, why was it me who went for the beer?

The war was over for Jim but not for me. I am going to stay alive even if I have to disobey orders.

After a few hours back at camp I queried the NCO asking him to explain why we were ordered to dispose of the mines in that way.

He told me to forget the incident and put it down to

an accident. I challenged him on the subject and asked was it right to be ordered to do something as dangerous and careless as we were ordered.

He could see I was angry so he pulled rank and told me to settle down and act like a soldier and get on with things.

I asked him if I could see the daily report to see exactly what had been said about the incident but he refused so I guess he would just log the event as an accident, when in truth we were ordered to complete a job we were not trained to do and should have been done by RE's, I believe.

One of the injured guys who I did not know sadly died during the evening and I was the only survivor uninjured as the other guy was badly hurt and had to be returned home. What really hurts is that Jim's Mum and Dad will get a standard telegram informing them that their son Private James Watson 14428202 5th Black Watch, 51st Highland Division was killed in action on 9th April 1945.

How on earth will they cope losing their only son?

One day, after all this horror has gone I will visit them and tell them what a great man he was and how proud I was to serve with him.

Right now I feel that the army see him as just another number and no one will ever know what he sacrificed for his country.

That night I did not sleep a wink. Things went through my mind over and over again about the incident and it's going to take a long time to come to terms with it. The next couple of days nothing happened, I got the feeling people around me were leaving me alone and allowing me to settle down.

On the 11th we moved to Ankum and on to Quakenbruke to take over from the Seaforths who had done a good job of clearing the enemy, taking prisoners, and allowing a bridge to be built over the river. We had no action, no incidents a clear run through. The Gordons were way ahead of us capturing small villages with little opposition.

It was not until we reached Dotlingen when we were attacked again, from a wooded area, but with massive support we drove them out of the woods and they retreated to a farm building.

After a minor attempt at defending themselves, within a short time they gave themselves up, there were about thirty of them including three officers.

The credit must go to the Gordons as they had fought for two days and we just joined in at the end.

April appeared to have flown by and it was now two weeks since Jim was killed and since his death very little had happened to make me feel threatened.

We had a few knocks and a few injuries, but most of the time we were just arriving at overcrowded concentration areas with lots of movements from all sorts of people.

There are Poles and Russians who have been used as slaves, now free to wander having been living in huts for the past few years, who are so happy and grateful whenever we arrive.

On the last day of April, news came that Adolf Hitler had killed himself. Now that is worth a celebration.

Apparently two days before he married Eva Braun then two days later committed suicide to avoid capture from the Red Army who wanted him alive.

We were told both Hitler and Braun ordered their bodies to be burnt.

This is great news, I was sure the war is over and I so wished Jim was with me celebrate this news. Definitely time for a dram or two.

We were transported further north without problems as it would appear any trouble was being sorted by the Gordons. They were in fact killing Germans whilst they are planting bombs, rather than finding bombs later. In each town we entered we would insist that the local Burgomaster gave us assurance that no soldiers were being hidden and if there were they must surrender.

Our superiors still maintained discipline and constantly reminded us to stay alert and remember our battle drills may still be needed.

Strict instructions were given about fraternisation with the Germans.

We should not humour them, joke, eat or drink with them, give them rations, cigarettes, or even shake hands, which is slightly contrary to the friendliness of both Jocks and Yorkshire folk.

Allied leaflets had been dropped telling all towns to

surrender, Bremen had been hit and flattened by our Lancaster's and Fortresses.

We had news that the Russians were about to take Berlin.

Gradually, day by day, the news came of mass surrender but still we were uncertain.

On the 8th May we were gathered together, just outside Bremerhaven to hear the official announcement that the Germans had signed the complete and unconditional surrender to the Allied Forces in Europe and the war in Europe was over.

The rum rations became available in unbelievable quantities.

The whole atmosphere is electric, we are relieved that fighting is over and everyone around us wants to celebrate freedom.

Parties are going on all over the place, girls are all up for anything. They want to dance, drink and just celebrate, much the same as we do.

We were brought back to reality when an announcement came that we must prepare for a victory parade through Bremerhaven and this is something our division take very seriously. Our kit was not in good order as we had battled for the last few weeks. Quartermasters issued cleaning kits to bring our kit up to scratch and we were ordered to polish everything, including our rifles which was something of a rarity. The parade was unbelievable. We lined up the width of the road, pipers led the parade until we paused as German Officers surrendered their arms to General Horrocks.

We were surprised at the lack of German spectators, they were still indoctrinated by propaganda and believed they would be shot for joining the celebrations.

Allied planes flew above us as we marched with our rifles over our shoulders, overcome with pride knowing this was a significant milestone in history.

This must be one of the finest days of my life.

Celebrations continued a huge bonfire was built in the main square and as the Jocks would say we partied into the "wee sma hours".

Hopefully the fighting is now over but there is still work to be done and we cannot let thousands of Nazi monsters to be allowed freedom.

We cannot allow those SS bastards and German Police terrorise the people of Germany who want to start a new life without the threat of Hitler upon them.

After a great time in Bremerhaven we moved about 20 miles away to a checkpoint over the River Weser. This is a key point to help control the movement of people. The bridge was the point where thousands of people had to cross if they were moving east of Germany. Bear in mind there were thousands of refugees, injured soldiers, people on the move carrying everything they had in old prams, suitcases bicycles, or anything else they could use. Amongst the crowds of free civilians were people who did not deserve to be free and it was our job to try and spot them, albeit we did this with little commitment as our war was over, we just wanted to go home.

The Field Police were keen as they constantly asked

us if we had spotted suspicious characters and if so they would be carted off to the guard rooms and eventually to internment camps.

On 22nd March continuing our boring task I was on duty with Corporal Tom Renouf, a friend of Jims dating back to Perth Training Camp, he was a bright guy from a very straight Scottish, Christian background.

He said "Come on let's see if they have anyone interesting held up in the guardroom."

As we sauntered in looking around at the many faces of interest, there was three guys sat in the corner and somehow they looked different to the others, very quiet when others in the room were chatting away. When questioned one of them became a bit aggressive leading to suspicion as he acted as if he was used to giving orders not taking them.

One of the men stayed quiet, he had a patch on his eye and dressed like a postman but somehow did not have the build and his clothes did not fit very well.

With hesitation, the would-be postman handed over his valuables, amongst those valuables was a very expensive looking wristwatch, not the kind of watch a working man would own or ever wear, he was also wearing an amulet.

The only reason he was in the room is because his paper work was too perfect as it claimed he was a former Sergeant

Due to Renouf's suspicious nature, the three guys were taken off to Barnstedt for further questioning.

During questioning the small man started to get angry eventually stood up, took off his eye patch, put on his spectacles and demanded to speak to the camp commandant.

The interrogator thought he recognised him as a German leader so he called his mate to get a second opinion.

His mate said, "It's bloody Himmler."

The interrogator said "I thought it was bloody Himmler."

At that point the small guy stood and shouted "Ich bin

Herr Heinrich Himmler."

Yes, he was indeed bloody Himmler.

What a catch, it took ages to sink in but they had captured one of the most important and wanted men in the world.

Headquarters were called immediately but initially they did not believe it, however Colonel Murphy travelled to Bremervorde where he found Himmler with the other two guys sitting quite relaxed.

He immediately found that the two guys were in fact bodyguards and they were removed to allow private uninterrupted talks with Himmler.

Himmler then got aggressive and demanded he spoke to Montgomery but British Intelligence drove him off to Luneburg.

After a short while using handwriting samples they concluded it was in fact Himmler and decided to progress to a medical examination conducted by Dr Wells. Himmler was not happy and during the examination he bit down hard on a concealed cyanide capsule already planted in his mouth.

The medical staff tried hard to flush out the poison but he was declared dead within minutes.

Himmler was probably the most wanted man in the world. He had fallen out with Hitler as he was judged to have failed his objectives and Hitler had already replaced him.

Himmler even attempted to open peace talks with the Allies but Hitler dismissed him and Himmler went into hiding.

Himmler was a bad man. On Hitler's orders he built the many extermination camps and was responsible for the deaths of many innocent Jews, Romani, Polish, Russians, how many exactly is unknown but it will account for millions.

A couple of days later I was talking to Corporal Renouf about his great achievement on spotting the suspect and he just said "It was a gut feeling and most of his observations came by looking into the eyes of people, simple as that."

He then said, "By the way, do you know when Nicky Nicholson took the valuables from Himmler and he had that fancy watch?"

"Yes", I said. Tom then slowly delved into his pocket and as he opened his close hand there it was: Himmler's watch.

I said "Where the hell did you get that from?" He said, "You know Nicky is a chain smoker and is always on the lookout for extra rations, well I don't smoke so I offered him 300 fags for the watch and he agreed. I think I deserve to keep this little treasure but I am not going to brag about it".

Germany is in disarray, although the war is over it's a confusing place to be as there is a lack of law and order. We are seeing looting not just from starving people but those stealing anything they can resell on the black market.

There are still revenge killings. Russians are not forgiving. There are confused Jews who cannot believe they are free and still in prison clothing. There are German civilians who still think we will shoot them. I have not met one German who has praise for their dead leader Adolf Hitler, it's as though he was their enemy. Maybe they are just covering their backs and afraid to speak truly.

It's going to take a long time for Germany to recover, I just hope I can get out of here as soon as possible.

Between the Allies and Germans we have wrecked the place and killed millions of people yet today I still cannot comprehend why this catastrophe had to evolve. 30th May. I just cannot believe the news I have just received, I will be returning to England on leave on 5th June and it may be possible I will not be returned to Germany but let's see.

6th June 1945. I am standing on the platform at

Kings Cross Station awaiting a train to Huddersfield via Wakefield and Leeds, in 2 hours' time I will be in Brighouse, I am so excited knowing Mum and Dad will be waiting for me.

As I look forward to my final journey I cannot help but reflect on the past and the experience I have shared with my comrades.

It has just hit me that today is exactly one year to the day that Jim and I landed on Juno Beach yet it seems like a lifetime.

Right now I cannot come to terms with the loss of so many comrades during the last 12 months. Am I lucky or did I stay out of trouble because I was never brave when things got heated.

Losing my best friend James Watson has taught me the true value of life but at the same time it has left me with a feeling of guilt as I have killed so many people. Now I know what it's like to lose someone you love and I cannot refrain from thinking how the families of those I have killed are suffering as I am right now.

How will I face Mr and Mrs Watson and James's sisters when I return? Should I tell them he was a hero and died instantly and embellish the good times yet hide the terrifying ordeal we have encountered?

I don't feel like a hero, I don't want to share my memories when I return, I am suffering from a great anticlimactic feeling, will I be able to return to the simple things in life?

I joined the army because that is what I thought was

right, maybe due to propaganda. They trained me to fight like a man for my country, they trained me to kill the enemy but what about the future, can we be untrained?

Will the army teach me to be a gentle, loving, caring person again? Will they help to release the torment in my brain or will I have to carry this heavy load for the rest of my life?

I am thinking, 'Will James go to Heaven? Will I go to Heaven? Will God forgive us for breaking the commandment:

"thou shalt not kill"?'

The 5th Battalion Black Watch was part of the 51st Highland Division, captured at St Valéry, June 1940.

It was reconstituted in Britain around the 9th Scottish Division. The remnants of the 1st Battalion were rebuilt and joined the 5th and 7th Battalions, going to

Egypt in June 1942. The Battle of Alamein, 23rd October 1942 engaged all three Black Watch battalions. The 5th Battalion was withdrawn from the front in November and was part of the forces pursuing the retreating Axis forces past Benghazi and Tobruk. Battles took place at Mareth, Wadi Zigzaou, Wadi Akarit, ending with Sfax, 9th April 1943.

Pipe Band of 51st HD Bremerhaven May 1945

Pipe Band of 51st HD Bremerhaven May 1945

Adolf Hitler committed suicide 30th April and Heinrich Himmler on
24th May 1945 after being captured by The 5th Black Watch

The dreaded Schu-Mine one of many types of mines
use by the Germans

INFORMATION ON THE 51ST HIGHLAND DIVISION

The 5th Battalion saw no more action in North Africa, moving to Algeria and training in amphibious landings for the invasion of Sicily, 10th July. From July until October 1943, the 5th battled and skirmished its way across Sicily and Italy. It was then sent back to Britain for training for the invasion of France. On 6th June 1944, it landed on Juno Beach, moving across northern France and Holland to the lower Rhine. It followed the 1st and 7th Battalions shortly after they had led the attack into Germany itself through the Reichswald on 8th February 1945. It crossed the Rhine on 22nd March under severe shelling, engaged in house-to-house fighting in Rees, and further actions until VE-Day.

The following table provides a brief summary of the

casualties suffered by the Division between August 1942 and the end of World War Two.

Campaign	Killed	Wounded	Missing	Total
North Africa	1,158	3,650	581	5,389
Sicily	224	910	301	1,435
Europe	1,702	7,487	577	9,766
Totals	**3,084**	**12,047**	**1,459**	**16,590**

The men killed alongside James on 9th April 1945 in Schuttorf, Germany. Taken from the 5th Black Watch ROLL OF HONOUR

Rank	Name	Number	Date	Place
Private	James Bruce	1798932	09/04/1945	Schuttorf
Private	David Finlay	13120189	09/04/1945	Schuttorf
L/Cpl	Thomas Hodson	2762246	09/04/1945	Schuttorf
Private	Daniel Strachan	1799085	09/04/1945	Schuttorf
Private	James Watson	14428202	09/04/1945	Schuttorf

JAMES WATSON'S RECORDS

James Watson is buried in Rheinberg War Cemetery
Germany Plot 13 Row B Grave 10

My dear friend Willi Paneutz took the time to find
the cemetery and drove me there following a business
meeting in Essen in 2003.

Part of the collection of James Watson's war records

1602166

The total possessions returned to James's parents included a torch, fountain pen, drawings, greeting cards, newspaper cuttings and a small Union Jack

PHOTOGRAPH ACKNOWLEDGEMENTS

I wish to thank the following for supplying photographic material.

The Watson Family

Janet Thomas

The Black watch Museum

Imperial War Museum.

Collection of Canada

Naval Historical Centre USA

UK Press.co.uk

German Federal Archives

Photos of War

Wikipedia

THE AUTHOR

I was born in Foleshill Road, Coventry on the 8th July 1946 just fourteen months after VE Day. Born into a Yorkshire family, my parents moved south to Coventry before the war in search of employment.

As a child, adult conversation would almost always include experiences of WW2 especially as we were still surrounded by bombed buildings.

It was bred into me to hate the Germans and this I believed until adulthood.

Coventry was an obvious target for the German bomb raids, due to its heavy metal-working industries including cars, bicycles, and aeroplane engines and munitions centres so the bombing started at the beginning of the war.

During November 1940, German 515 Bombers and Heinkel aircraft hit Coventry in the most severe raids experienced throughout the war. In one night alone more than 4,000 homes were destroyed, including the cathedral, police stations, two hospitals and many churches. Around 600 people were killed and over 1,000 injured in just one day.

My mother lived through the war with three children; it must have been a terrifying experience living in those rows of terrace houses, some of which had been hit.

As children, bomb sites were the playgrounds of the day and we would re-enact the battles using blocks of wood for rifles.

Despite being very poor there was a great feeling of community spirit, everyone helped each other, we did not know how close to poverty we were as everyone else was poor.

I was christened James because I was the next child born into the family and my mother had lost her only brother, James, while he fought in Germany. I was seen as special child to all my aunties, uncles and grandparents due to the loss of James. I became a replacement, almost like James reincarnated, to the point where my grandfather wanted to adopt me and take me to Yorkshire, the birthplace of my parents.

I have always had some kind of affinity with James, sometimes I feel as if I know him. Maybe it is because as a child when visiting my grandfather I would play with James's toys in the attic.

In 1956 the family, now five children, moved back to Yorkshire following the death of granddad Albert Watson.

In the 90's I was called to a meeting in Enschede in Holland and after a heavy night of drinking I was involved in a shocking car accident in which we wrote off a new BMW as it somersaulted over a ditch and rolled into a field.

I got away with bumps and bruises. I had no idea until much later that the accident happened less than 10 miles from where James was killed.

A few years later I was at another meeting in Essen in Germany and I could not stop thinking about James, affected by a weird feeling that I was close to where he was in action. On studying a map later, I was indeed less than 15 miles from where he is buried in Rheinberg War Cemetery.

So at my next meeting in Essen I found time to visit the cemetery and found James's grave where the four boys killed on the same day were buried together side by side.

I don't believe in Heaven and I don't believe in Guardian Angels but there is something there that I do not understand.

From then on I decided to start to research exactly what went on and what happened to James. There was little communication available in 1945 and as a result his family know just about nothing on the subject, yet today with the internet it is much easier to research. I want the memory of James to live on in future generations and to this end I decided to write this book and, with the help of many kind people and various museums, I believe this story to be an accurate record of his involvement in the war effort.

Despite my humble beginnings, I became relatively successful in business having had eight years as a young executive with Asda, been director of a couple of companies and finally started my own business in 1990 until retirement in 2006.

During those years I visited Germany on many

occasions and eventually formed strong business relationships with German customers and made lifelong friendships with many.

In conclusion, although having witnessed the results of war and being brainwashed into a hatred of Germans, in adulthood I realise that the Germans are just ordinary people who experienced just the same pain as the British during the war years.

I no longer hate the Germans. I admire and respect them immensely.

Printed in Great Britain
by Amazon

22204873R00145